Julie Jo Fehrle

Jonathan Lethem

THEY LIVE

JONATHAN LETHEM is the author of eight novels and five other books of fiction and nonfiction. His writing has been translated into thirty languages, and he has received many awards, including the National Book Critics Circle Award, the World Fantasy Award, the Pushcart Prize, and a MacArthur Fellowship. Lethem lives in California and Maine.

Deep Focus

Deep Focus

They Live

Jonathan Lethem

Series Editor, Sean Howe

Soft Skull Press | New York

Library of Congress Cataloging-in-Publication Data
    Lethem, Jonathan.
They live / Jonathan Lethem; edited by Sean Howe.
        p. cm.—(Deep focus)
ISBN-13: 978-1-59376-278-0
ISBN-10: 1-59376-278-X
1. They live (Motion picture) I. Howe, Sean. II. Title.
PN1997.T4275 L48 2010
791.43'72—dc22

                                        2010013025

Cover design by Spacesick
Interior design by Elyse Strongin, Neuwirth & Associates, Inc.
Printed in the United States of America

Soft Skull Press
An Imprint of Counterpoint LLC
1919 Fifth Street
Berkeley, CA 94710

www.softskull.com
www.counterpointpress.com

Distributed by Publishers Group West

10 9 8 7 6 5 4 3 2 1

For Giuseppe Sorrentino

It's one of those peculiarly impoverishing gifts that popular post-modernism has bestowed on textual (so to speak) analysis—scatter clues on the surface (intertexuality, "symbolism," ironic juxtapositions, etcetera) like so much flotsam and you, the reader/viewer/listener get to say "Hey! I think there might have been a shipwreck here! If only all those Coast Guard cutters and Air-Sea Rescue helicopters would get out of here so I could study these signs more closely!

—CHRISTOPHER SORRENTINO

Carpenter has been in the past a conservative director. But there's no mistaking the film's satiric intent, which he expounded upon in his interview with [Lewis] Beale. There Carpenter linked Reagan's presidency to "fascism" and "the rise of the fundamentalist right and the kind of mind control they're putting out." Oddly, Carpenter underestimated his audience intellectually while overestimating them economically by concluding, "My prediction is a few folks will get [the allegory], but most will say: 'What is he talking about? Is he talking about me?' Then they'll get in their BMWs, drive home, take off their expensive clothes and Rolex watches and slip into their Jacuzzis and say, 'Nah, that's not about me.'" For whatever it's worth, both times that I saw *They Live*, the audience seemed to be fully clued in to what the film was about, and I sincerely doubt that any of them owned a Jacuzzi . . . In fact, the movie is a confusing blend of anti-Reagan satire and genre conventions that make the film every bit as crass, amoral, and mulishly blinkered in its many rightwing assumptions as the attitudes it is ostensibly attacking. It all adds up to an ideological incoherence that is rather suggestive in relation to the recent president election.

—JONATHAN ROSENBAUM,
"Liberals Kick Ass," *Chicago Reader*

I think the real question about *They Live* is why it's so great *despite* its baldly obvious satire of '80's consumerism. *They Live* is beyond scholarship. —ANDREW HULTKRANS

These unjust and scornful remarks are easily understandable. Their motives lie in the reactionary commentators' sense that they themselves are the zombies so acutely exposed and satirized in the movie. It is this feeling of those who not only do not understand, but do not wish to understand, that stirs their indignant contempt, and not any concern to show some real shortcomings of the film which, if existent, are definitely of secondary nature . . . Asked if his approach is somehow related with Marxism, Carpenter answered in the negative. Nevertheless, *They Live* does not cease to be perhaps the Marxist movie *par excellence* in the history of the seventh art. Even if it appeared 20 years ago, it does not cease to be topical and will remain so until the social evils it so graphically and skillfully depicts will be removed through social transformation.

—CHRISTOS KEFALIS,
"When Science Fiction Meets Marxism," *Dissident Voice*

"As soon as I get back I'm going to tell my superiors all about this *fucked-up* planet." —NATASHA HENSTRIDGE,
in John Carpenter's *Ghosts of Mars*

They Live

What You'll Recall of the Dream in the Morning

A street preacher's warning and a pirate television broadcast.

The demolition by riot policemen, helicopters, and bull-dozers of an open-air homeless-persons' compound in a vast vacant lot. A brazen assault on a ghetto church.

The hero, a wrestler garbed as a construction worker.

A pair of sunglasses that reveals yuppies as alien ghouls.

A chilly, enigmatic beauty, her intentions toward our hero unknown.

The black guy and the white guy. They begin in distrust, but soon learn they've got enemies in common. From that point they'll cover each other's backs.

Machine-gun fire in a television studio.

A surprise with tits.

But, above all, two sequences:

One, when the wrestler first dons the sunglasses and, exiting an alley, walks through a city revealed. Ten minutes of cognitive dissonance as sublime as anything in the history of paranoid cinema, shot partly in black-and-white, and composed with the serene assurance of Hitchcock or Kubrick.

Two, a fistfight in that same alley: crass, bruising farce stretched to an absurd limit, wagering the film's whole stakes decisively on a pop-culture/"termite art" bet.

Note on Approach I

This is the first monograph on *They Live*. My apologies for not offering production details, or for not placing the film in the context of John Carpenter's oeuvre, or within the science-fiction or horror-film genres per se. I didn't interview Carpenter, or anyone else close to the filmmaker's process. I *did* read everything I could find written on the film: not much. If you're in the camp that sees Carpenter as a master auteur, you'll think the existing literature on his career is appallingly scant. If you believe he's an errant journeyman, you'll be amazed to know he's attracted scholarship at all.

My first encounter with a Carpenter film was *Dark Star*, at a mideighties campus screening. I loved it. Then, years later, I played catch-up, with VHS tapes and, later, DVDs. My interest was intermittent, and frequently disappointed. I've never seen a John Carpenter film in the theater except *Memoirs of an Invisible Man* (which, because I'd relished the H. F. Saint novel that was its source, I found thin and toneless). Like a lot of people, I think 1982's *The Thing* is his "best" film, but I probably adore *Dark Star* and *They Live* just as much, and I've got a weak spot for *Escape from New York*. As that list suggests, I find Carpenter more compelling as a science-fiction (or science-fiction-horror) director than I do in his "official" role as Master of Horror. In the years when I took Carpenter most seriously as an auteur I labored to find *Halloween* and *Assault on Precinct 13* "interesting"—well, they are interesting, but they didn't interest me so much that I've ever gone back to them. Two or three of his films I've never managed to see, and I'm not worried about it.

After a strong beginning, Carpenter's role as an auteur has a somewhat fizzled-out quality to it. Or is that the "auteur approach" gives diminishing returns lately? Recent candidates for that kind of enshrinement accumulate less evidence—Carpenter's seventeen features in thirty-six years to, say, Don Siegel's thirty-six in thirty-six. So it may simply be easier now to read individual films than whole careers. Anyway, without wanting to give Carpenter short shrift, I'll do my best just to read the film. In the vanity of my aspirations, I'd do for *They Live* what Raymond Durgnat does for Hitchcock's *Psycho* in *A Long Hard Look at "Psycho,"* but that isn't really possible—not only because I don't have anywhere near Durgnat's vocabulary of film analysis at my fingertips, or because *They Live* isn't at *Psycho*'s level, or because I lack Durgnat's number of pages. Though all these things are true, the more important obstacle is that Durgnat was able to read *Psycho against* hundreds of other readings and responses—the broad but also deep cultural resonance *Psycho* has attained by now. By that standard, I'm working in the margins, in the dark. I may not be literally the first person to put on these glasses, but it *feels* that way.

Note on Approach II

A Netflix copy of *They Live* plays behind these words as I type. Not on a television screen in the same room, but on the computer screen, on which my document also appears. Thanks to contemporary technology—not just DVDs, but YouTube excerpts, available via the wireless signal in the café where I write sometimes, if I've forgotten to bring the disk—I'm Pauline Kael's ultimate opposite here: I've watched the entirety of my subject film a dozen times at least, and many individual scenes countless times more (Kael used to brag of seeing each film only once). This situation isn't normal in the history of film studies (unless it's "the new normal," which it probably is): even if Robin Wood or Tag Gallagher resorted to owning a 16-millimeter print or a VHS tape of their Hitchcock or Rossellini subjects, they'd have worn holes in those artifacts and perhaps also destroyed their projection devices with the kind of obsessive close viewing I can do simply at the click of a cursor.

They Live, known generally as a "cult" film, lends itself to obsession. Howlingly blatant and obvious on many levels— some might ask, *How many levels do you really think there are?*—it grows marvelously slippery and paradoxical at its depths. Some days I hate the thing, for a while it bored me completely. But it came back, too. I watched *They Live* with friends, letting it do its work on new victims—that was one way to refresh myself. Needless to say, I began spotting details no one would register at a first viewing. In fact, I began spotting details few would register at a fifth viewing, or a tenth, such as the fact that the homeless blond "man-boy" Nada rescues at 27:15 is the same person from whom he borrows binoculars at 20:50. Maybe John Carpenter knew that once, but I bet he's forgotten it.

Watch something enough times and all you see are the holes, much like a word whose meaning dissolves because you've said it aloud too many times in a row. I'll spend a lot of pages describing what's oblique or paradoxical or simply contradictory in *They Live*'s material, not in order to expose the film, but because those gaps are usually also closely related to its richest provocations, its vibrant ambiguities; it wouldn't be wrong to say that its gaps are also zones of pregnancy, the places where the film is hatching what I think is most worth wondering over. According to the concept of "suture," every movie (short of single-take exceptions like *Russian Ark*) consists of papered-over gaps, in which the language of narrative film stitches together unrelated elements—shots, but also meanings—to present the illusion of unity. Out of holes, a whole.

I'm rambling, but the point I want to make here is that I genuinely like *They Live* (which has nothing to do, of course, with ascribing every virtue, or for that matter every defect, I locate within it to some absolute agency on the part of its maker or makers). I'm sure I'll watch it again, even after this vigil is concluded. If we meet up, I'll watch it with you. In the meantime, I think you'll have fun with this book—or, hey, *without* this book—if you watch *They Live* yourself.

Note on Names

I'll call the figures in the film by their character names when describing their actions within the diegesis (which is most of the time), and name the actors only when remarking on their performance, or their life and career outside this film in particular (which is less often). So "Nada" rather than "Roddy Piper" (though both, as it happens, are fictional names), and so forth.

One of *They Live*'s eccentricities is that we know Nada's name only because of the end credits. No one speaks it in the course of the film. Yet his name is hardly incidental—Nada's name, with its implication that he's something of a zero, or null-set, turns out to come directly from the Ray Nelson short story "Eight O'clock," *They Live*'s primary source. Similarly, the irascible homeless man/turncoat called "Drifter" is only granted that nickname by the credits. Most significant, while the film takes (laborious) pains to indicate that the creatures revealed by the sunglasses are *aliens*—i.e., science-fiction creatures who've invaded from another world, by means of advanced technology—the credits dub them *ghouls*. And they really do look like degenerated humans—like zombies, or decaying corpses, or perhaps corroded humanoid robots or cheapo androids. Don't they? (This contradiction, this tension, isn't incidental.) As with Nada's and Drifter's names, I'll take my lead from the credits, and call the things ghouls.

Note on Diegesis and Ideology and Peekaboo

I'll try to hold the line on jargon, but I need these two words: *diegesis* and *ideology*. *Metatextual*, too. Take this, for instance: "Despite being a film that sweats metatextual implications from every pore, *They Live*'s *diegesis* is uncommonly sturdy, unpressured by actual *metatextual* gestures." In fact, this tension between the film's simplicity and its strangeness, between its thunderous stolidity and its abject porousness, is probably what compels me most. No offense, but *They Live* is probably the stupidest film ever to take ideology as its explicit subject. It's also probably the most fun.

Speaking of ideology, all I mean by *that* word is more or less what Roland Barthes refers to in his introduction to *Mythologies*: "The starting point of these reflections was usually a feeling of impatience at the sight of the 'naturalness' with which newspapers, art and common sense constantly dress up a reality which, even though it is the one we live in, is undoubtedly determined by history. In short . . . I resented seeing Nature and History confused at every turn, and I wanted to track down, in the decorative display of *what-goes-without-saying*, the ideological abuse which, in my view, is hidden there." *Hidden*, that's the key word. My efforts here, like *They Live* itself, are energized by the gloriously rudimentary pleasure, not, I suspect, unknown to Roland Barthes, of peekaboo: the giddy thrill of unmasking what may from some vantages be regarded as howlingly obvious, yet goes by common consent unspoken.

Note on Notes

This book has notes, unnumbered, at the rear. Look there for (further) attributions, informal bibliographic remarks, gossip, speculation, dubious parenthesis. Or don't; they're relegated for nonessentiality. No texts were harmed in the making of this text.

The Opening of the Eyes

(0:00)

> Going to the cinema results in an immobilization of the
> body. Not much gets in the way of one's perception. All
> one can do is look and listen. One forgets where one is sit-
> ting. The luminous screen spreads a murky light through-
> out the darkness. Making a film is one thing, viewing a film
> another. Impassive, mute, still the viewer sits. The outside
> world fades as the eyes probe the screen. Does it matter what
> film one is watching? Perhaps. One thing all films have in
> common is the power to take perception elsewhere.
> —Robert Smithson, "A Cinematic Atopia"

A dream or nightmare is underway: out of darkness an ominous, admonitory phrase resolves, in hand-lettering, under the
director's name. John Carpenter's *They Live*. The black fades
up to a graffitied wall, on which the title phrase takes its place
in a chaos of urban, spray-paint cartoons. It's atypical, "un-
realistic" graffiti, featuring too many childish drawings—of
what look like public-housing projects, a floating hypoder-
mic syringe, a monumental Christian church—and too little
flamboyant font. The wall seems flat, a "title card," just for an
instant, then a leftward pan claims it as an element in a location shot: an overpass in a train yard. The camera's movement
halts, shifting the title phrase nearly offscreen to the right.

But the viewer's ability to calculate what's moving and what's still is complicated by the rightward drift of the train cars that now center the frame (and, in a film that will concern various kinds of public language, bring with them their own odd phrase, SHOCK CONTROL).

So: a triple optical confusion in thirty seconds of screen time. A warning—matters of competence in "reading" images will be at stake here. Now, the camera movement and the passage of the train act as sliding doors to reveal our hero, Nada, played by the possibly recognizable-to-some nonactor (or aspiring actor) "Rowdy" Roddy Piper, professional wrestler.

Garbed in default blue-collar duds and wearing a backpack, Nada picks his way out of the distance, across the tracks, toward us. Like Toshiro Mifune in *Yojimbo*, or Randolph Scott or Clint Eastwood in any number of American or Italian Westerns, our hero strolls into the story's frame through civilization's back doors, unnoticed, an entrance simultaneously suggesting modesty of means, self-reliant competency, wraithlike anonymity, and (at least to begin) neutrality as regards any preexisting conflict.

We can't be certain, but Nada's probably been riding the rails. In any event, what he does from this point is *walk into Los Angeles*.

Los Angeles Plays Itself

"Every film is a documentary of its actors," declared Godard. The same is true of cities, according to Thom Andersen's *Los Angeles Plays Itself*, an essay-film on the subject of Hollywood's inadvertent enshrinement of Southern California settings as backdrops. *They Live* shows up in Andersen's documentary as a typical example of how the city idles in the background, candidly disclosing itself to whatever eye may care to notice. Carpenter's film neither declares its Los Angeles setting as a subject nor troubles itself to conceal it. Denver and Detroit are mentioned in passing, default locales for an out-of-work white guy and an out-of-work black guy, respectively, but the Los Angeles to which they've migrated goes unnamed. Still, the Los Angeles Athletic Club is visible in several shots. Various other buildings are framed long enough to be identified, but they're mostly unmemorable. Carpenter avoids—or can't afford—anything as distinctive as the Bradbury Building's interior. His use of L.A.'s downtown feels documentary itself, in the helpless manner dictated by the film's low budget.

The most distinctive location in the film isn't architectural, per se: the blasted rise on which the homeless compound Justiceville has assembled itself, and from which it will shortly be cleansed by an army of bulldozers and riot police. I asked Thom Andersen for more on this location's history: a marginal zone west of the Harbor Freeway, it had in fact been cleared by speculative developers in the late seventies and early eighties precisely to make way for more of the luxury towers contemplated by Nada and Frank as they gaze across the freeway in the distance. So, *They Live*'s urban-renewal subtext embeds a bit of real urban history, knowingly or not. According to Andersen, the planned towers never exactly showed up. When the area filled in, it was with cookie-cutter, middle-class condominiums.

Left unengaged is Los Angeles's car culture; apart from the police, no character seems to even *own* one until Nada kidnaps Holly Thompson (Meg Foster) in the garage where she's parked. The L.A. of *They Live* is dominated by foot traffic, and not only that of the homeless, but also of the boisterously populated streets around the newsstand, grocery store, and bank. *They Live* ignores the presence of the film industry, too. The alien broadcast emanates from a *TV* station, eliding Hollywood, the official U.S. Dream Factory (the equivalent of setting in New York City a film about mind control, but ignoring Madison Avenue). Television is one of *They Live*'s preoccupations, but there's no acknowledgment of the thin line between film's and television's production culture.

In fact, Roddy Piper, as a wrestler, could be seen as a version of the TV star who's attempting to move into feature film. Traditionally, that's something like a baseball player trying to jump from the minor to major leagues: a routine attempt, but still carrying a hint of embarrassing hopefulness, and no guarantees. Nada never uses his decoding sunglasses to peek at a movie marquee, to see whether the title of, say, *Good Morning, Vietnam*—the top-grossing movie in the months during which *They Live* was filmed—might translate to *Sentimentalize War*.

Bum-Bum-Bum, Waaah-Wah

The musical score's entrance performs its own sleight of hand: documentary train-yard noise resolve seamlessly into a drum tick, so we can't be sure where one leaves off and the other begins. John Carpenter's most celebrated eccentricity may be his insistence on composing his own scores, which tend to feature an idiot savant repetitiveness, along with synthesized sounds that, to some ears, date badly—a thrifty man's Tangerine Dream. I treasure them, myself.

They Live's score may be the most tauntingly circular in film history, short of *The Third Man*'s zither or *Eyes Wide Shut*'s one-finger piano: a rootsy but menacing three-note bass line, ascending and descending along a blues scale, joined by taunting saxophone and a long-suffering, rueful, old-man harmonica: *Bum-bum-bum, waaah-wah*. Drum and synth join to raise the pulse when cops or guns walk through the door. The bass line is ominous enough to claim "something's happening here," undercut only by the harmonica's rebuke: "same old, same old." Ultimately, the blues motif telegraphs the film's underlying air of nihilistic resignation. It lightly mocks Nada's (and the viewer's) panic at the film's revelations. *You knew this already, didn't you? No? Really?* (Or, as Nada groans when he glimpses the Reagan-ghoul, "It *figures* it would be something like this.") If the film's opening evokes some kind of homeless advocate's public-service documentary—or at least an attempt at blue-collar vérité, like Charles Burnett's *Killer of Sheep*—the music warns that it may skip past ordinary fiction to become a kind of fuck-you cartoon: *Waaah-wah!*

Bums

(2:18)

In the movies, homeless people—or street people, or dere-
licts, or bums—sometimes get to play the lead in egalitarian-
redemptive comedies like *My Man Godfrey*, *Trading Places*,
Down and Out in Beverly Hills. Elsewhere, they're the common
castoffs worth saving, or sanctifying as salt-of-the-earth: *Meet
John Doe, Sullivan's Travels*, *The Grapes of Wrath*, *The Soloist*.
They can also be terrifying, a ready, invading horde of the
hungry and desperate, a kind of quasi-zombie army, or a more
individual specter or nightmare, a negative mirror or id vision
of the self's potential degeneration: think *Ghost*, or *Mulholland
Drive*, or Carpenter's own *Prince of Darkness*.

Though the indigent in *They Live* will eventually be played by actors, or obvious extras (including a few comically implausible candidates for the street), the first few we glimpse below the credits are more than persuasive, sheltering themselves from the rain with broken umbrellas and cardboard crates or plastic tarpaulins, massed indifferently on street corners and with belongings clutched in paper sacks or garbage bags. They're also (unlike the actors and extras) all black or Latino. Mostly black. The degree of verisimilitude seen here is probably out of reach of *They Live*'s costume department and production design—that is to say, its budget—so we can feel pretty certain Carpenter's nabbed a few oblivious conscripts for these shots.

By exhibiting these folks, *They Live* pushes its political context to the foreground, reminding us there's something or someone to be noticed in plain sight (at least for urban audiences). Nada, for his part, is technically homeless, but wants and finds work. In general he seems to float a little apart from the despondently indigent population so visible in the film's first half hour. In his self-reliance, alertness, and industriousness, Nada, when introduced, may recall more the kind of marginal but indomitable blue-collar type played by Humphrey Bogart in *The African Queen* or *The Treasure of the Sierra Madre*. The question for that sort of character isn't how he'll ultimately find bed and board, but whether he'll either find a way out of his contingency and isolation to marriage and collective affiliation (*African Queen*), or descend into paranoiac dissidence (*Sierra Madre*). Carpenter compulsively cites the apolitical camaraderie of Howard Hawks as his model, but

John Huston's splintered alliances and cynical-leftist nihilism is a lot closer to what we're given in *They Live*.

Carpenter shot the film in March and April of 1988; *They Live* was released that November. In the summer months between, Tompkins Square, a small park in Manhattan's East Village, erupted in riots—a series of semiviolent stand-offs between city authorities and the homeless occupants who'd made the park an equivalent of *They Live*'s Justiceville. It was at the Tompkins Square Park riots' height that the invective chant "Die, Yuppie Scum!" (*They Live* distilled to a bumper sticker?) was invented. Within a year, *Die Yuppie Scum* was not only a graffiti standard, but was also a T-shirt, and "Meet me in Tompkins Square" was a refrain in a Lou Reed song. I suppose you could take this as confirmation that *They Live* grokked *somebody's* zeitgeist.

The parallel has its limits, though. Tompkins Square Park was marked, as Justiceville isn't, by defiant drug use, by countercultural—mostly punk-rock—signifiers, and by overt and quasi-political defiance (cops being taunted as Nazis, etcetera), as well as by the presence of protestors and interested witnesses from the ranks of the middle-bohemian class (including Allen Ginsberg). *They Live*'s homeless are sheepish, demoralized, obedient, and stripped of signifiers of dissident affiliation or criminal ambition. Apart from seeking to get themselves fed in *Grapes of Wrath*-style grub lines, they're content to zone out and ponder television. They'd climb inside those screens if they could, much sooner certainly than they'd mass at barricades.

By depicting the homeless of Justiceville as exclusively weary and long-suffering (akin more to L.A.'s own Rodney

"Why-can't-we-all-just-get-along?" King than to the chip-on-their-shoulder flash-mob at Tompkins Square), Carpenter's made certain that Justiceville's destruction can be read only as Darth Vaderish totalitarian overkill. The real threat to the overlords is in the small adjacent church, not the open-air homeless shelter. Demolishing a neatly quarantined homeless preserve serves no purpose (unless these bulldozers are clearing the way for development). In fact, it would likely displace these unsightly humans into other neighborhoods, much as the Reagan-era dismantling of the psychiatric-service infrastructure flooded urban zones with those formerly under treatment for full-blown mental illnesses.

Ironically, in the same era in which political sensitivity was demanding *bums* be re-euphemized as *homeless persons* (a shift, like *drunk* to *alcoholic*, from something verbishly active [*I'm bumming, I'm drinking*] to something nounishly passive [*I endure homelessness, I suffer alcoholism*]), the uncomfortable fact was that a highly visible layer of the people on the street in the 1980s was manifestly crazy, paranoiac, seeing things or hearing voices. Yet Carpenter's homeless are placid (except in the case of the dyspeptic Drifter, a reactionary sellout waiting for his chance). Blind preachers and down-on-their-luck construction workers *see* things; the homeless see only televisions. The rebel manufacturers of Hoffman lenses inside the church will never for an instant consider distributing those potential instruments of prole revolution among their immediate neighbors in Justiceville. Better the revelatory sunglasses molder in cardboard crates than be wasted on those losers.

Auteurs within Auteurs

Nor is it to be thought (ran the text as Armitage mentally translated it) that man is either the oldest or the last of earth's masters, or that the common bulk of life and substance walks alone. The Old Ones were, the Old Ones are, and the Old Ones shall be. Not in the spaces we know, but between them, they walk serene and primal, undimensioned and to us unseen . . . He knows where They had trod earth's fields, and where They still tread them, and why no one can behold Them as They tread. By Their smell can men sometimes know Them near, but of Their semblance can no man know, saving only in the features of those They have begotten on mankind; and of those are there many sorts, differing in likeness from man's truest eidolon to that shape without sight or substance which is Them. They walk unseen and foul in lonely places where the Words have been spoken and the Rites howled through at their Seasons. The wind gibbers with Their voices, and the earth mutters with Their consciousness. They bend the forest and crush the city, yet may not forest or city behold the hand that smites.

—H. P. Lovecraft, "The Dunwich Horror"

The words "Directed by John Carpenter" mark the director's third appearance in the credits (after the possessive over the title, and the music credit with Alan Howarth). But if we're in the know, we'll recognize the screenwriter "Frank Armitage" as a Carpenter pseudonym, plucked from the pages of H. P. Lovecraft's "The Dunwich Horror." As we've learned an instant earlier, *They Live* is "Based Upon the Short Story 'Eight O'clock in the Morning' by Ray Nelson." For those inclined to trace such connections, Ray Nelson, an (extremely) minor writer even within science fiction's demimonde, was one of just two people with whom Philip K. Dick ever collaborated on a novel. So: lurking unnamed in these credits, like secret masters, are Lovecraft and Dick, perhaps the preeminent ontological para-noiacs of twentieth-century fiction—also two now-esteemed artists situated, like Carpenter, in disreputable genres.

"The Dunwich Horror" doesn't feel much like *They Live*. Lovecraft's story is (typically) both purple and morose, full of crypto-historical cobwebs, and a million miles, tonally, from Carpenter's urban setting, media satire, and neo-Hawk-sian buddy-picture motifs. What "Armitage" seems to have glommed from "Dunwich," apart from a general fascination with the invisible omnipresence of mankind's enemies, is the ominous indeterminacy of the pronoun *they*. Lovecraft's secret masters are octopus-headed devils from an ancient realm, as uninterested in dressing up in yuppie costumes and shopping for blue-corn tortillas as can be imagined.

Employment Agency

(3:05)

They Live's first official scene puts Nada at the desk of a dourly sarcastic employment counselor. He's there just long enough to sketch his sketchy backstory (ten years working in Denver, then "things just seemed to dry up . . .") before being dismissed: "There's nothing available for you right now." Adding to the efficiency of the one-minute scene's portrait of no-trickle-down economic times, a droning announcement comes over the loudspeakers: "Due to a computer error, the food stamp program has been suspended until further notice . . ." A one-legged man in a wheelchair—*A veteran?* we might wonder, though he lacks the ironic military uniform and Willie Nelson beard-and-ponytail of the prototypical embittered Vietnam vet—shakes his head grimly as he exits, exasperated at some slight he's endured therein. Employment agencies usually turn up in films where matters of work will remain central—*Straight Time, Lost in America.* Nada, however, solves his job problem within three more minutes of screen time, adding to our impression that his self-reliance sets him apart from the crowd. This scene is, like the homeless people, meant to set political context, rather than to describe where this particular protagonist is coming from or bound.

Watching the film a second time, a viewer begins to wonder which other characters would have been unmasked as ghouls had Nada worn the sunglasses from the start. The employment counselor makes an interesting first candidate. She's both distinctly shriveled and heavily coiffed and made-up. These, together with her skeptical, almost sneering response to Nada's remark about banks closing, evoke the ghoul-in-furs Nada will meet at the grocery store. As we'll see, older female ghouls evoke such a degree of revulsion from Nada that it borders on ghoul misogyny. Yet she's more likely just a sarcastic and unsavory crone—such people do exist, after all. Take it as a small first vote in favor of the view that we earth folk were capable of being unappealingly lousy (or, unappealing *and* lousy) to one another well before any alien intervention.

Outside the Limit of Our Sight, Feeding Off Us, Perched on Top of Us from Birth to Death, Are Our Owners

(3:50)

The blind, black street-corner preacher candidly "reads" *They Live*, for those who'll listen—which is no one, not yet. It comes too early and too fast for any of his rhetoric to really sink in. Anyway, the literal warning is veiled in a religious-metaphorical mode here—the problem with transmitting such local and acute knowledge by means of Bible-thumping is that its speaker will seem a boy who cried wolf. How often have we had to ignore apocalyptic pronouncements from guys sounding like him, over the years? Nada seems dubious. If anything, he's impressed that the cops would bother with this guy. Mostly, having sniffed out conflict, he looks eager to disassociate himself: like *Casablanca*'s Rick, he came only for the waters; never mind that he was misinformed.

"Rowdy" Roddy Piper

> Nakedness is presented as *metaphor* rather than truth, and it implies that even this monolithic image can be subliminally transformed and acquire new and contradictory meanings. Here it suggests that there is no privileged truth to be found in the pose—the "gesture"—of the body builder played by Schwarzenegger. The matter is open and ironic, as art ought to be.
>
> —Mark LeFanu, on Bob Rafelson's
> *Stay Hungry*, in *American Directors*, Vol II

Roddy Piper (a stage name for Roderick George Toombs) will remind nobody of Humphrey Bogart, really, despite all my insinuations. Or even Clint Eastwood. He's a professional wrestler, representing a minor stop on Hollywood's journey from Johnny Weissmuller to The Rock. (Ours was, of course, the movie era where Schwarzenegger and Stallone proved how decisively a weightlifter turned actor trumps an actor turned weightlifter: the former goes from laughingstock to box-office-champ to Governor of California, the latter from Oscar-winning character actor to washed-up oil painter.) Under Carpenter's hand, Piper wears his aspirations lightly, seeming barely to have shrugged off his other career for these duties. That said, he isn't bad. As you'd expect from someone with hundreds of hours' experience playing opposite other professional wrestlers in what is essentially live, semi-improvised theater, Piper's best in scenes opposite Keith David or some other strong male presence, worst in his scenes with Meg Foster or other women. Piper is the blunt tool this job requires: conveying fear and rage is in his wheelhouse.

"Unlike most Hollywood actors, Roddy has life written all over him." This, John Carpenter's explanation of his casting choice, expresses a typically masculine discomfort with the fakery and costumes of acting. Like much to do with *They Live*, the remark embeds a matter-of-fact dichotomy—us against them, "life" versus acting—while begging us to tease out the buried ironies: the "life" Piper has written all over him is his life as a famous, straight-faced *fake*. Anyone wearing the glasses of good sense knows that pro wrestling *is* acting. Yet unlike "real" actors, who willingly take off their disguises and discuss the secrets of their craft, professional wrestlers—like *They Live*'s ghouls—will never admit their deception except amongst themselves, unless forced at gunpoint, or perhaps under sworn testimony.

Piper, with his slight acne scarring and not-intolerably-leaden vocal delivery (including occasional slips into a Canadian accent) makes a fair token of the real. If he knows how funny it is that he should be asked to act shocked at finding himself in the *unmasking* business—since pro wrestling involves both frequent unmasking at one level, and the persistent refusal to be unmasked at another—he keeps it mostly to himself. The exception will be the alleyway fight scene, where, allowed to unveil his "real" life expertise in "fake" hand-to-hand combat, a teasing irony plays over Piper's expressions. More on this later.

Television Made Me What I Am

(4:49)

"Wake up! They're all about you, all *around* you . . ." Cutting on these words from the preacher, the film shifts to a grainy-video montage, playing on what turns out to be a wall of tele-visions tuned to an identical channel: Mount Rushmore, an eagle on the wing, a Native American doing an "eagle" dance, a rodeo cowboy barely clinging to a bucking bronco, a toddler dressed as a cowboy falling off a bucking sheep, and a group of white guys on a basketball court, celebrating victory with sweaty high-fives and backslaps. As the pan and zoom-out reveal the television as part of the contents of a shop window, facing the street, we learn the cut has neatly concealed an eli-sion of hours: day given way to night, the first that Nada is to spend in Los Angeles.

Our hero moves along, barely interested. But these televi-sions have completely hypnotized a viewer on the sidewalk, a young and neatly groomed black guy. By appearances, this street man's probably not homeless, yet he seems spellbound by the distance between himself and the American imagery offered up onscreen, which will reveal itself, an instant later, as being broadcast from "Cable 54." The creepy montage, merely a signature promo used between programs, begs inter-pretation: all the Western iconography, and those two pairs of *real* and *ersatz*—the actual eagle and the costumed Indian, the "real" cowboy and the pretending child—as well as the obnoxiously hearty white guys kicking ass on a basketball court, the appropriation of totems (the Native American's eagle, the black man's game), and the totemization of appropriators (those Mount Rushmore heads). Does Carpenter want us to question the Anglo-European claim on North America? Apparently so.

Television screens *are* all around us in *They Live*'s first half hour. They're the "purloined letter"—that which hides in plain sight, the thing we can never quit seeing and not seeing. In a sense, the screens serve as the film's placeholder "monsters in our midst" ("our masters," as the preacher puts it) until the true faces of the ghouls are made visible. Once Nada dons the sunglasses, the television screens mostly fade out of the frame (at least until the film's last moments). But they'll have served their purpose—not only in keeping us disturbed, but in telling us how to feel about the ghouls' easy interpenetration of our daily lives. Sci-fi monsters *might* just be this insidious and seductive. Maybe we'd welcome them into our homes, or pine for them through shop windows, or sit and watch them in a vacant lot. In fact, the residents of Justiceville are seen watching television just before their encampment is bulldozed, and again first thing the next morning, while they pick through the rubble.

What Carpenter places on these screens is rarely again quite as concentrated or haunting as Cable 54's corporate montage. But the satirical slant is, well, slanted. Three of the four television broadcasts glimpsed—at 5:23, 11:50, and 29:11—consist of broad swipes at eighties consumer-celebrity brainwash. An aspiring actress ranting orgasmically about her dreams of a fame that will take her up like Christian rapture: "And I never never get old, and I never die!"; a commercial for glue-on fingernails as ludicrous as a *Saturday Night Live* parody, if less funny; and a hideous primary-color fashion catwalk with voice-over narration like Orwell-out-of-*Interview*-magazine: "Oman's collection puts passion before fashion. Dash and trash are back. Out goes glitter and in comes *divine* excess. The fall collection *revels* in freedom of expression . . ." Carpenter gets away with the jeering, *Mad*-magazine hostility of these satires because they're handled as passing glimpses.

The only piece of "real" appropriated footage comes at 13:30: a glimpse of a black-and-white creature feature, Jack Arnold's *The Monolith Monsters*. In the snippet we see, titanic crystalline pillars collapse as though imploded to crush (obviously miniature) cabins below. A line of dialogue, "they're pulling the water out of the sand like sponges," distills every blandly ineffectual movie scientist who ever faced down an extraplanetary invader.

No matter how ominous, the grainy "reality effect" of this footage seems to call up a better, deeper world than that of the satires of contemporary television around it. One of the functions of films like *The Monolith Monsters*, in the fallout-shelter fifties, was to insert contemplations of death into an atmosphere of remorseless cheer, just as part of film noir's duties was to open up a space for the despair of returning World War II veterans in a culture that didn't want to hear about it. Here, the fifties are made to seem a whole lot deeper than the eighties. At the very least, a black-and-white Jack Arnold movie is something John Carpenter certainly likes (it's a *movie*, for one thing), in a world drowning in his obvious dislikes (television commercials, and the kind of television that might as well be a commercial). Seeing the old movie, and probably liking this kind of thing ourselves, we lean forward.

Using *a fine theatrical feature film like the one you're watching* as a club to beat up broadcast television isn't original to *They Live*, of course. Carpenter's dabbling here in one of the generic motifs of midcentury Hollywood: a self-regarding distaste for the rival medium of television, that "vast cultural wasteland." The adoption of TV sets into the middle-class home—a genuine mass social transformation—is portrayed, time and again, as a kind of minor-key tragedy. Television, according to the movies, is an opiate brain-washing machine, largely associated with either numbed housewives or emasculated husbands, or as appropriate to the mental level of eight-year-old boys pantomiming cowboys. Never will anything vital or surprising be glimpsed; life is elsewhere.

The absurd apogee of this theme comes in Douglas Sirk's *All That Heaven Allows* (1955), where the gorgeously lonely widow Jane Wyman is prematurely put out to pasture—shifted to a status beyond reach of sex or adventure—by her anxiously conformist progeny's introduction of a brutally massive color television into her living room. Take that, Mom! As late as Don Siegel's 1976 *The Shootist*, a deliberate elegy to John Wayne and therefore to the studio era per se, Wayne's dying gunfighter must first shoot down a pair of famous television cowboys—Hugh O'Brian, formerly TV's Wyatt Earp, and *Have Gun, Will Travel*'s Richard Boone—before succumbing to a bullet himself. Siegel's film argued, implicitly, that the 1950s television cowboys who might have been seen to usurp Wayne's place in the culture never even came close. The grudge, twenty years later, was that fresh.

Has it been put to rest even now? Darren Aronofsky's *Requiem for a Dream* (2000) subjects Sirk's appliances-as-feminist-nightmare motif to a particularly grotesque expansion, gathering up the fridge along with the television. *They Live*, with David Cronenberg's *Videodrome* (1983), Paul Michael Glaser's *The Running Man* (1987), and Paul Verhoeven's *Robocop* (1987) and *Starship Troopers* (1997), demonstrates that feature film's vigilance about TV-as-lobotomy has hardly relaxed. Really, why should it? The kettle may in fact be black, even if the pot's the one pointing it out. But interrogation of this theme has moved "underground," as it were, out of middle-class melodrama, into the safely exaggerated and dismissible zone of science fiction (or, in the case of *Requiem for a Dream*, drug hallucination), like satires of the Soviet Union slipping past Soviet censors.

Union Sundown

(5:59)

Nada lands his construction-site job in a brief and loaded exchange with a hard-hatted, middle-aged foreman. The foreman hedges when asked if they "need anyone"—"Maybe," he replies, "but this is a union job." He and Nada together glance at a group of Spanish-speaking workers, apparently slacking and goofing off at the edge of the site. What seems an undignified swipe at organized labor bears at least a trace of storytelling purpose: a chance for Nada to demonstrate his wiles, since he's quick enough to ask to see "the shop steward."

From an eighties left-politics perspective—to which the anti-Reagan theme would seem to commit the film—this cynicism about unions is troubling, even creepy. It's about as coherent a statement as Bob Dylan's 1983 "Union Sundown" ("Sure was a good idea / 'Til greed got in the way"), a song that gave jitters to those who still wanted to believe Dylan was in the Pete Seeger column. In another few scenes Nada and his new construction-worker friend, Frank, will have a chance to extend the film's intricately muddled lumpen-critique of the workingman's plight. For now the union reference just sits there, seemingly gratuitous.

As usual for Dylan, his real theme on "Union Sundown" was apocalyptic and timeless, not any kind of scrupulous poli-sci take on current events. For John Carpenter, too: both seem to be saying that the corrupted nature of contemporary life means any man seeking his way in the world walks a valley strewn with pitfalls, or thorns. "I've got my own tools," Nada assures the foreman, an invitation to wonder how Christian a figure this wandering, quasi-carpenter is destined to become; a suffering protector with a special claim on truth who'll at the last instant be betrayed, then sacrificed for his cause. Yet it won't be Christ we're thinking of when, a moment later, Nada doffs his shirt.

Gay Porn

(6:37)

Nada's black, construction-worker colleague, Frank, played by Keith David, sidles up to the topless hero, then arches his eyebrow and purrs: "You need a place to stay? Justiceville's over on Fourth Street. They got hot food and showers. I'm goin' there if you want me to show you." At this instant the universe divides between those snorting popcorn through their noses and those others who'll be affronted by the suggestion that there's anything sexual in the air. But we can let the precedent of the wildcat literary critic Leslie Fiedler's homosexual decoding of *Huckleberry Finn*—"Come Back to Raft Ag'in, Huck Honey," (and what's Huck Finn if not the prototypical black-guy-and-white-guy buddy saga?)—set the pick for us here. If we don't need Mark Twain's permission, we don't need John Carpenter's.

What makes this exchange feel winky-nudgy? Partly it's the fluffy excess of Roddy Piper's musculature, so smooth and top-heavy, so unlike that of the actors and extras he's surrounded by, so unlike a real construction worker. Partly it's the sweet-beneath-the-gruffness gift of Keith David's expressive face, and the burnished and insinuating Barry White quality of his vocal delivery. But even more, it may be that the low-budget vagueness of the movie up to this point is *already* reminiscent of a porn film, specifically of pornography's typical interval of stalling before getting down to its horny business. If we've even half-consciously registered some uneasiness about the film's purposes, we might now be tempted to think that maybe it was *that* kind of business, now underway at last.

If it's not that kind of hookup scene, it's still a hookup scene. In the scenes of blue-collar banter that immediately follow, Nada and Frank strike a mutual spark, swapping if not bodily fluids then back stories and dumbbell aphorisms ("He who has the gold makes the rules," "The middle of the road's the worst place to drive," etcetera). We may or may not recognize Keith David from *The Thing*, or from one of his other half-memorable roles before or since. Though he works incessantly, David's one of those character actors you might have trouble fixing in mind, being a bit more talented than Ernie Hudson, a shade less weird than Bill Duke, and far less regal than Lawrence Fishburne—and his two-first-names doesn't offer any mnemonic help. Yet it's obvious that from here on we've got another hero besides Nada in this story, someone likely to stick around.

The Black Guy and the White Guy, Together Again for the First Time

We've been watching this movie our whole lives, with minor variations. It provides something we need at the bluntest level, an assuaging counterexample to the fact that, when we look around us, the white guy and the black guy mostly *aren't* together. If it's Eddie Murphy cast opposite the white guy then the black guy's the dominant star, which maybe tweaks vicarious guilt (on the part of the white viewer) or compensatory fantasy (on the part of the black viewer) even more thrillingly. If he's Will Smith there's a risk he's Bagger Vance, the dreaded Magic Negro, offering redemptive guidance on the white guy's more essential voyage. Most often, though, he's Danny Glover, in what we might, in tribute to *Miami Vice*, call the Tubbs Placement: just a tad behind the white guy in significance and charisma, perhaps a bit slower off the blocks or on the uptake, but situated alongside his white compatriot in a gallant role distinguished from the villainous or colorless figures that otherwise populate the story. No doubt that's where Frank's headed. It's not the *worst* place in the world.

Individual Ethics under Late Capitalism

(9:48)

While the white guy and the black guy gaze at the distant towers of wealth, they ponder. Frank's bitter worldview encompasses a zero-sum social Darwinism: "They put you at the starting line, and the name of the game is make it through life, only everyone's out for themselves, and looking to do you in at the same time." Nada, devoid of the black man's inevitable shoulder-chip, ignores the bait. He offers stoic, if vague, solidarity: "I believe in America . . . Everybody's got their own hard times these days." In political terms, Nada's an innocent—does he think the occupants of those distant towers have their "own hard times"?—while Frank's a cynic. For the narrative, a nice twist is in the works: Nada will eventually have to bludgeon his black friend into seeing the truth Frank seemingly already possesses.

Hacker

(12:01)

A rebel "hacker," professorial in his glasses and white beard, breaks into the television show being enjoyed by the homeless in their outdoor living room, which consists of discarded chairs and an upturned spool for a coffee table. We'll see him twice, at night and sometime the following day, suggesting that this particular group of indigents rarely budge from the boob tube. " . . . A small group of scientists who discovered, quite by accident, the signals being sent . . . Keep us asleep, keep us selfish, keep us sedated."

As with the street preacher, the hacker lays out the situation and the stakes plainly, even predicting *They Live*'s ending: "The signal must be shut off at the source." Yet his message, larded through with both static interruptions and monotonous political-speak, is tempting to reject as leftist cant (much as high biblical style made the preacher easy to ignore): "They are dismantling the sleeping middle class," "They have created a repression society, and we are their unwitting accomplices," etcetera. What the hacker never does is *identify* the threat: aliens, ghouls, or otherwise. The incantation of the pronoun *they* conspires with the film's title, more disturbing in its encompassing vagueness than any monster's name.

The homeless do reject it, with irritation. Nada, standing by, has started to suspect something. He glances in the direction of the church. There we see the street preacher lip-synching the words of the hacker's broadcast, even pausing when the signal fails, as though "channeling" this radical feed. The unnerving detail is never explained. Unless we're fumbling around in the neighborhood of ESP, or choose to believe the street preacher is some sort of robot with a signal receiver in his forebrain, it *can't* be explained, except by the suggestion that, as with the blind prophet Tiresias, or Marvel Comics' Daredevil character, the blind are granted uncanny compensatory powers. Anyway, the cutting from this weird motif back to the fuzzy pirate broadcast, then to the black-and-white *Monolith Monsters*, creates an eerie montage, full of visual and sonic dislocations—one of *They Live*'s "art film" moments, for sure.

Truth Hurts

The involuntary witnesses to the pirate broadcast all concur: "Thing's giving me a headache." Not for the last time, knowledge in *They Live* is associated with head pain, grogginess, and eyestrain. Nada hasn't even tried on the glasses yet and he's already seen pinching the bridge of his nose and wincing. It's more comfortable not to see.

Gilbert, the garrulous ambassador to Justiceville, has another reaction. At 15:37, he can be seen leaning in to watch the broadcast, then anxiously twiddling an imaginary knob as if trying to resolve the image when it fritzes out in static. Like the street preacher, it pains Gilbert when the signal *fails*.

Fake Church Conspirators

(16:40)

Nada's chosen to investigate. He slips inside the church in a framed-in-silhouetted-doorway shot that makes conspicuous reference to the iconic entrances and exits of John Wayne in *The Searchers*. The image is ostentatiously reinforced at the back end of the sequence. Does this nod to John Ford serve any deeper purpose than reminding us how much John Carpenter likes Westerns in general, and embittered loner heroes in particular? Well, for one thing, Nada's stumbling onto the fact that there's a posse in this town. As with Wayne in *The Searchers*, this is a posse he'll join, but with reservations, and from which he'll (typically) end up disaffiliated, riding solo.

Now Nada discovers a reel-to-reel tape recorder, which is being used to create the illusion of a choir of churchy, testifying voices. (Here's a kind of confession of how film audio and image might be routinely combined to spare low-budget film-makers the expense of dozens of extras.) It's worth noting that while the unmasking of ghouls is the film's primary motif, the first fakers Nada unmasks are playing for the *human* team. We also see another kind of graffiti, an indoor slogan apparently painted with a narrow paint roller, reinscribing the film's title within a larger slogan: THEY LIVE, WE SLEEP. Given its location, this bit of advertising can only be for the benefit of those already in the know, a piece of intra-resistance cheerleading, like a coach's message pinned to the locker-room wall.

Inside the temple, the bearded hacker, Gilbert, and a black conspirator argue over the efficacy of the broadcasts versus other activities generated by their revolutionary cell: "robbing banks," or "manufacturing Hoffman lenses until we're blue in the face." Moments later, the black preacher catches Nada fumbling in the church, after their secrets. He tells our hero that "it's the revolution," and, when Nada nervously begs off, assures him, "you'll be back." These three—hacker, preacher, and Gilbert—bear secrets: the hacker and preacher eager to share theirs, Gilbert trying to cover his. So, it's not too shocking to discover that all their secrets are one and the same. But what are Hoffman lenses? And what's with the fly-by-night chemistry setup? At a glance, it looks like a meth lab. Nada fails to connect it with those cheap-looking plastic sunglasses Gilbert and his cohort don in order to examine the prowling helicopters.

Assorted Hoffmen

Some commentators on *They Live* credit "Hoffman lenses" as a reference to the accidental discoverer of lysergic acid diethylamide, or LSD, the Swiss chemist Albert Hofmann. This makes an appealingly hip reference to matters of delusion and revelatory insight—the sunglasses as a kind of "windowpane" into reality, including a twist: What if hallucinations, once induced, revealed the fact that ordinary consciousness was itself a mass hallucination?

There's another pretty fun candidate: Abbie Hoffman, subversive yippie jester and fugitive, and a paragon of "us versus them" political stances. Among Hoffman's legacies is his terrific 1967 stunt in which he hurled paper currency from the gallery of the New York Stock Exchange onto the trading floor, interrupting the smooth operation of money-grubbing with an outburst of money-grabbing. What was this if not an attempt, very much in the spirit of *They Live*, to expose the dollar's *E Pluribus Unum* motto as *This Is Your God*?

I'd rather end my report there, but according to the website Realnews247.com, *They Live*'s sunglasses were named in honor of the holocaust denier Michael Hoffman II. Brief lesson for paranoiacs: setting your open-ended conspiracy metaphors loose upon the world, they become (like anything) eligible for manifold repurposing. Free your mind and an ass may follow.

Hoffman lenses have become one of *They Live*'s free-floating signifiers, a talismanic high sign to be flashed by admirers.

The term was taken for their name by a Canadian reggae band, and inspired the punk band Set Your Goals's "With Hoffman Lenses We Will See the Truth." Replica Hoffman lenses were also, as recently as 2007, available from the merchandise page of Roddy Piper's personal website, though last I checked the link was dead, the page removed. Someone doesn't want you to get your hands on these!

Drifter I

(20:03)

"I've been hearing somethin' on the streets the last couple of weeks. *Weird* stuff. Some sort of epidemic of violence, is what they been saying. I was talkin' to one old boy, he's from, uh, San Anselmo. He told me they got some sort of cult up there. End of the world kind of stuff . . . You know, shootin' people, robbin' banks. Same old thing as always. Whole lot of people gone *crazy* over some nutty dream they just had. You want to know the truth? This kind of shit happens the end of every century. It does. It's just people afraid to face the future, it's all it is."

—Drifter

A homeless denizen of Justiceville, named in the credits as "Drifter" (and fourth-billed, overall, after Nada, Frank, and Holly), has begun to distinguish himself. As with Nada, no other character calls him by this name—perhaps it seemed too telling to speak aloud, since Drifter's special place in the film will be to make an unlikely passage from one realm to another seem as effortless as drifting with the tide.

Played by a pet actor of Carpenter's with the marvelous name of George "Buck" Flower (beginning with 1980's *The Fog*, Flower appears in five Carpenter movies), the drawlingly jaded Drifter seems more irritated than unsettled, both by the hacker's interruptions in his television shows and by the rumors of disquiet leaching down from San Anselmo, even as he propagates them himself. With his squashed hat and Members Only jacket, he seems a bit too vain and self-possessed to read as homeless or indigent; he reads more as a no-good husband kicked out by some Roseanne Barr-ish wife, or maybe just a free-range couch potato.

Drifter's role in the film expands stealthily. At first introduction he barely registers, partly because his muttered conspiracy-mongering is intercut with foreboding shots of the gathering assault on Justiceville: the hovering helicopter casing out the fake church, and Nada, patrolling from the hillside with a pair of borrowed binoculars, like Nick Nolte in *Who'll Stop the Rain?* By the end of the sequence, evening's creeping in, and Nada's still watching. We feel something coming, nearer now than San Anselmo: a millennial "epidemic of violence" or collective "nutty dream," or, maybe, some combination of the two.

Villainous Vehicles

(22:40)

The demolition of Justiceville is more than a tableau of urban renewal in fast-forward—it takes on the quality of sci-fi nightmare. The filmmaking methodology is in the spirit of the Jean-Luc Godard of *Alphaville*, or the George Lucas of *THX 1138*, who forged their "futures" out of alienated modern urban spaces. Who needs Terminators when your wide-angle lens can frame helicopters and bulldozers for maximum techno-angst? Riot gear turns the phalanx of L.A. cops into another kind of machine, a collective chewer or thresher, before the battle breaks down into sporadic commando sniping. Score-wise, churning synthesizers now overrun the homely bass-and-harmonica blues, reinforcing the John-Henry-versus-the-Steam-drill feel. Remember Mario "put your bodies upon the gears" Savio? Tonight, the gears are winning.

Carpenter, who directed Stephen King's *Christine* (a murderous 1958 Plymouth Fury) shows a special relish for the menace lurking in mechanical transport. His favorite villainous vehicle is the helicopter: Nada will later be killed by a sniper shot from one. Helicopters hound the noble alien visitor in *Starman* and the Invisible Man in *Memoirs of an Invisible Man*, and they usher in the Thing's arrival in that film's opening sequence. But there's a twist: Carpenter himself is a helicopter buff, and he rarely missed a chance to climb aboard.

He's credited as "Man in Helicopter" in several of his films. So, in *They Live*'s ironclad us-versus-them scheme, the director's affiliation with his persecuting machines points to a subliminal ambivalence, or even complicity. So far as helicopters go, John Carpenter's one of *them*.

Disruptions, Discontinuities, Departures

In the chaos of the attack, we may or may not find time to note these:

The first police vans to arrive bear the label SCIENTIFIC IN-VESTIGATION, though the cops are certainly pulverizing anything that might resemble evidence.

Drifter's reaction, while others flee, is that of a detached observer; he smokes a cigarette and squints. Then, when others either fight or run, he stands before a phalanx of riot cops with an expression of appeal, as if hoping to negotiate his surrender. This quietly telegraphs Drifter's slippery affiliations.

Oddly, since the blind preacher seems eccentric to their conspiracy, Gilbert and the hacker usher him across the street as though he's their top priority. (They've already emptied the church of cartons full of sunglasses, apart from that one box they've helpfully left behind for Nada to discover). Does the spiritual dimension of their (seemingly political and scientific) campaign of resistance mean more to them than they're willing to admit?

Nada and Frank become separated in the mayhem, but tenderly, as if after a lover's quarrel.

The raid appears at first to be directed at the church. Then attention turns to the destruction of Justiceville. If the conspirators have seemed indifferent to the connection between these two zones, the police link them in the attack. Nonetheless, the church is left undemolished—were the bulldozers inadequate for taking down an actual building?

In Justiceville, the morning after, though scraps of clothing and other possessions are strewn throughout the flattened lots, the televisions still work (the fashion-show broadcast must emanate from some extra-diegetic realm).

Life During Wartime

(26:26)

With Justiceville under the hobnail boot, its population scattering, Nada bears witness as the hacker and street preacher are cornered by riot police and beaten into silence. Whether they'll survive this assault seems questionable; certainly they're neutralized as far as any organized resistance is concerned (and out of the picture, quite literally—we never see them again). On the fringe of this grim tableau, Nada takes pity on a blond, age-indeterminate fellow who's cringing, immobilized by fear (the man-boy from whom, earlier, Nada borrowed a pair of binoculars). Nada and his ward take refuge inside an abandoned apartment, one stocked, for added pathos, with a filthy discarded child's doll. There, they join with the blond father and daughter who'd been watching television with Drifter (gathering in one place the movie's three least-convincing actors playing homeless people). The way this kid responds to Nada suggests he's meant to be read as a teen runaway, despite the fact that he looks too old to qualify as a teen; it's only in his extreme deference to Nada's sheltering bulk that he seems boyish. (More gay porn.) Only later, learning as we will of Nada's traumatic childhood, may we wonder: Does Nada see in this kid some version of his younger self?

Inside the ruined apartment, they encounter a squatter: a dazed black guy smoking what looks like just a smoldering marijuana joint, though the whole ambiance here screams "*crack house*." "Come on in and join the party, man," says the squatter, persuasively desolate. "Somebody start World War III?" Nada, peeking through uneven, film-noir slats at the devastation, looks properly rattled. He makes no answer to the squatter's remark, which, left reverberating, reads not only as bleakly cynical, but as effective "political" information: for those like *me*, the squatter might be hinting, World War III (a *class* war?) is a given. Nada's come late to the "party": he's just received his draft notice.

Half-Hour Mark

(30:00)

The morning after the raid, as the strains of the last TV show fade, the homeless pick through Justiceville's rubble. Nada crosses the street, walks into the now abandoned church and, in many ways, into another film, one in which he'll switch from observer to active protagonist. So much fades, so quickly: farewell to the homeless and their horizontal encampment, with its overtones of the Western, its mess lines and campfires—the remainder of this film is to be played amid urbanites and their vertical buildings, those we've been regarding from a contemplative distance. A cut at 30:50 smashes Los Angeles's geography: Nada rounds the corner of the church and emerges into the mouth of an alley in a downtown neighborhood. He won't look back.

When Nada tries on the glasses, the ghouls become visible, desublimating the film's subject, making an obvious revolution in his, and our, experience. Less obvious is the fact that Nada has abruptly become visible himself. Up to this point he's slipped like Kurosawa's Yojimbo past any official gaze: policemen and their helicopters seem not to register his comings and goings, and he's made little more impression on the resistance leaders (ironically, the only one who "saw" him was the blind preacher). From here on, he's legible to both camps.

Just one thing remains to heavily cue continuity, precisely at this half-hour mark, as Nada frisks the church to find the hidden crate of sunglasses, then migrates into a whole 'nuther mise-en-scène: *Bum-bum-bum, waaah-wah!*

The Next Six (or Eight, or Ten) Minutes of Film

Desert island time: Carpenter's *The Thing* is his masterpiece, and I can easily think of two dozen directors I personally hold above Carpenter. But, given the imperative to preserve just a dozen sequences from film history in a time capsule, the rest to evaporate from human memory, I might pick the next six, or eight, or ten minutes of *They Live*. I'd pick them to stand for the eighties, and for the minor tradition of the "self-conscious B-movie," and for that side of science-fiction cinema devoted to what the critic Darko Suvin calls "cognitive estrangement" (as opposed to wish fulfillment, thrills, action, techno-lust, or horror). And I'd pick them out of affection. This, for me, is *They Live*'s hard, chewy, delicious center. If I had the powers, I'd slow these minutes down and expand them, somehow, into a world in which to linger and explore like an interactive DVD or video game—flipping through more of the "translated" magazines, gazing at the revelatory architecture and signage, eavesdropping on further conversations. I'll try the next best thing, slowing my little book down to dwell here, to savor the sequence from as many angles as I think it can tolerably sustain. (I believe it can sustain more than a few.)

So—six minutes, or eight, or ten? I know where to begin: in that alley. Up to now, the film has been an explosive device in assembly, one painstakingly accumulating the force, the plastique, of implication, needed to detonate when Nada takes his new sunglasses for a walk down the street. *They Live* is never so pressurized again; how could it be? Exploring the new world this sequence leaves behind, the film is destined to wander through smaller recursions of the same eureka moment, through action-film braggadocio, through dumbbell sci-fi explanations, nervous violence, and grating in-jokes. No complaint from me: what came before has earned it all. But if *They Live*'s "masterpiece sequence" falls back to earth, exactly when is it? And how? I'll audition candidates for this stopping point as I come upon them.

Cheap Sunglasses

(31:18)

Nada's disappointment, when he discovers that the illicit or subversive treasure he's salvaged from the church turns out to be a carton full of sunglasses, may or may not be a conscious joke about the film's low-budget props: the first unveiling of futuristic technology being something available in any drugstore for a few dollars (exact price depending on whether these are brand-name Ray-Ban Wayfarer glasses or a knockoff—I can't find confirmation one way or another, but would bet on the knockoffs). Ray-Ban Wayfarers, which convey an iconographic lineage back to J.F.K. and Marilyn Monroe, as well as Audrey Hepburn in *Breakfast at Tiffany's* and Cary Grant in *North by Northwest*, had been established as a specifically eighties movie icon by a crushingly effective product-placement campaign begun in 1982; after Tom Cruise's use of the glasses in *Risky Business* (1983) and Don Johnson's in *Miami Vice* (1984–89), and then with their adoption by the music icons Michael Jackson and Debbie Harry, and in the texts and jacket designs of the novels of Bret Easton Ellis, the glasses were an eighties cliché no one was ever embarrassed to deploy. *They Live*'s original promotional poster must have been a conscious satire of the poster for *Risky Business* (it's less likely the designer had the sleeve of Elvis Costello's *Trust* in mind).

Still, when they're added to Nada's blue-collar uniform and trucker haircut, a mild degree of code-switching is in the air. In a breakdown comparable to the early sixties U.K. mod/rocker binary, Wayfarers, together with suits and ties, and short-back-and-sides haircuts, suggested a new-wave stylistic glancing back, past the hairy seventies, to late-fifties cool. Nada's look, signifying country-hippie or heavy-metal grit, evokes blue-collar disdain for all that's urbane; his type's more likely to be decorated with aviator frames, perhaps with reflective lenses. Once he adopts the glasses, Nada's scruffy-with-Wayfarers look calls up one droll referent—ZZ Top, who sang: "Now go out and get yourself some big black frames / With the glass so dark they won't even know your name . . ."

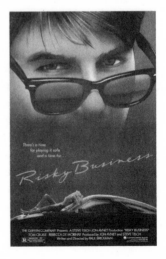

The Mad Flaneur

(32:07)

> As newcomers swarmed into the cities . . . anonymity
> became a condition that almost everyone experienced at
> some point during the day—in a remote *quartier*, visited
> for the first time on business; on an unknown street, turned
> down by mistake; in a neighborhood encountered in the
> morning rather than the afternoon . . . Thus, a proposition:
> what cannot be read threatens. The first sites of this new
> anxiety were Paris and London, vast metropolises where
> people could disappear without a trace, where (as in Balzac
> and Dickens, the great chroniclers of the potential anonym-
> ity haunting all urban identities) credentials, antecedents,
> and even names became suspect.
>
> —Robert B. Ray, *How a Film Theory Got Lost*
> *and Other Mysteries in Cultural Studies*

Rounding the corner, out of his alley and into the (surpris-
ingly, for Los Angeles) bustling urban promenade, Nada becomes a walker in the city, a flaneur or boulevardier, yet one
for whom the ordinary premises of urban coexistence are immediately about to dissolve. Anonymity's a mutual bargain for
privacy; you're not supposed to, as Woody Allen joked about
the metaphysics student taking a final exam, look "within the
soul of the boy sitting next to" you. To do so is to go mad;

such degrees of involuntary insight are conventionally intolerable (hence the traditional retreat of super-empathic creatives, the Vincent van Goghs and J. D. Salingers, from the affective maelstrom of the metropolis). Or, in the words of Jim Morrison, "People are strange when you're a stranger." (No one remembers your name, Nada.) Seeing too much means glimpsing the corruptions hidden from ordinary mortals: perhaps, in that case, you're Sherlock Holmes, uniquely competent to perceive the signs of Moriarty's evil. The answer, then, is to become a detective. Alternately, you may be, like Miss Lonelyhearts in Nathanael West's novel of the same name, destroyed by your knowledge of suffering. The alternative to madness, in that case, is art.

What makes *They Live* political is the irreconcilable distance between the revelations visible through the Hoffman lenses and the placid surfaces of everyday life. The ghoul conspiracy *too completely* invalidates the point of view of those excluded from knowledge: no detective or artist can fix what's wrong here. Acts of detection disturb everyday life just locally and sporadically, by removing the problem of the criminal element. Art does the same thing, by addition instead of subtraction: the "ordinary" is revamped or redeemed by effective imaginative gestures.

In *They Live*, everyday life itself is Moriarty. Revolution is the only reply. What makes *They Live* a comedy, and a tragedy, is Nada's inadequacy to this insight: he's qualified only to become a creature of instinctive rage, stranded between knowledge and wisdom, or between a fact and its implications. Once he knows *they live*, he never knows another thing.

But first, before Nada gathers in the fact of the ghouls, our flaneur finds himself stranded in a world of denatured signage. (*They Live* is an entertainment that sneaks in a lesson in reading, an episode of *The Electric Company* for grownups.) The commands Nada encounters on the billboards and at the newsstand may seem fairly straightforward, once we've recovered from the jolt of their uncovering: OBEY, SURRENDER, STAY ASLEEP, WATCH TV. Yet some commands are easier to obey than others. Nada's abilities to CONSUME are sharply limited (he's rarely seen with so much as a dollar in hand, and the only nourishment he'll gather during the film is a soup-line handout). As for our homeless construction worker's hopes to MARRY AND REPRODUCE, these look as likely as his hopes of vacationing in the Caribbean. Maybe Nada, our so-called ordinary Joe, *is* a freak like Sherlock Holmes or van Gogh after all: if he *wished* to conform, he'd still have problems. The only distance longer than that between our (enforced) desires and their disguises may be that between desire and satiety. It's enough to drive a man on the street mad.

They Colorized It

In *They Live*'s scheme, color is lies, black-and-white the truth. This links the world the Hoffman lenses reveal to *The Monolith Monsters*, that black-and-white creature-feature movie seen earlier, and to an era of stripped-down and formally pure cinema Carpenter fears is being overrun by the ethos and aesthetics of the yuppie-Reagan eighties. Later, during the brief resurgence of the anti-ghoul revolutionary cell, a background voice is heard exclaiming indignantly, "They colorized it!"—a film buff's in-jokey reference to the outrages then being perpetrated by Ted Turner's TNT channel upon helpless black-and-white classics, begun in 1985 with the Michael Curtiz-directed James Cagney musical *Yankee Doodle Dandy*. The elegant framing and slow cutting of *They Live*'s black-and-white "revelation" sequence, together with the welcome evaporation of the musical score, reminds us of Carpenter's capacities for, and commitment to, a classical mise-en-scène; again, and for the last time now, we're watching an art film. In fact, the shot that climaxes the pre-ghoul half of this revelation sequence—the "impossible" matte-painted cityscape seen at 33:29—recalls nothing so much as the wide shot of the disturbingly placid, shadow-painted gardens in *Last Year at Marienbad*.

Black-and-white is the color of "evidence," as in police photography, or the iconic scrutiny of death in Mathew Brady or Weegee; documentary filmmakers like Frederick Wiseman

held off on color long after fiction film had mostly succumbed to it. Related notions of purity held sway in the fine arts until photographers like William Eggleston broke down barriers against color processes that had been stigmatized as both untrustworthy and vulgarly middlebrow. *They Live*'s black-and-white sequence is joined by eerie camera crawls, and the sound track is quiet precisely because the film has "fixed" the world, in the manner of a crime scene, in order for us to read it.

At the height of the colorization crisis, a rumor spread that Ted Turner intended to colorize the Kansas sequences in *The Wizard of Oz* (actually, he restored them to their original sepia). *Oz*, one of *They Live*'s small cohort of films using black-and-white and color for contrasting effects in the same diegesis (see also Godard, Spielberg), counterpoints dream and awakening, circa 1939; audiences might be accustomed to reading Depression "reality" as black-and-white, while color, offered in a scant minority of thirties film, remained circumscribed in fantasy. By 1988, the contrast inscribes a paradox, one that unmasks despair at the core of Carpenter's nostalgia. Dorothy might draw viewers "back" to the embrace of dusty old Kansas, sure. But, straddling *that* dream and *this* reality, to what sanctuary might Nada hope to retreat?

Luckily, in this update the Wizard's handing out not hearts or brains, but automatic handguns.

Impossible Eloquent Cityscape

(33:29)

> "If you're driving down a street, going up in an elevator, or
> sitting in a restaurant, you find that your eyes travel around
> the room at a specific height . . . if I'm watching a scene
> I'm interpreting it through my eyes, so where I will put
> the camera is wherever I'd like it to be. It doesn't mean it's
> right; it just means it's mine."
>
> —John Carpenter, quoted in *Boulenger*, John Carpenter

For one tantalizing instant we're treated to a wide shot of a
sunstruck Los Angeles desublimated: under lengthening afternoon shadows, dozy vehicular traffic courses beneath vast
billboards reading SUBMIT, STAY ASLEEP, and CONFORM.

The shot's composition is futurist-sublime—this may be the nearest we'll come to wishing to submit to *They Live*'s poisonous trance. In fact, here the film subtly ruptures our identification with Nada, leaving us to meditate alone with our masochistic ache for authority's loving grace: though the suturing action of shot/countershot suggests this wide shot proceeds from Nada's Hoffman-lensed view, the angle on the traffic is far too high to be that of our man on the street. We're looking *down* at the traffic. As if, in a dream, we've soared free.

Graffiti and Text Art

Sometimes it was as simple as thinking of people I knew and trying to write a version of what came out of their mouths. The reason I wrote from every point of view—Far Left, Far Right, common-sense, lunatic—was that I thought it was a more accurate way of portraying people's beliefs, and maybe a better way than always having didactic or dogmatic stuff. I thought that—and this is utopian—it might be a more effective way to have people consider these issues and not turn them off. A lot of times when something is identifiably Right, or Left, the people who agree with it will agree with it, and the people who don't will dismiss it instantly. I thought it might be more mysterious and less off-putting if a universe of opinion were laid out, with all sentences equally weighted—which in a way is a sign of respect for the audience. Each person coming to this universe will have to find his or her way through it.

—Jenny Holzer

In the early nineties, first in Providence, Rhode Island, and then up and down the eastern seaboard, thousands of paper, and later vinyl, stickers began proliferating in the urban commercial-detritus/graffiti collage of lampposts, subway entrances, and construction-site billboards. The stickers presented a blunt little graphic, a visage of testosteroid hostility, recognizable to some as the masked face of the professional wrestler Andre the Giant, accompanied by various slogans—most often ANDRE THE GIANT HAS A POSSE.

After a 1994 lawsuit denied use of the wrestler's name, the reworked stickers took up a *They Live* theme: the wrestler's face was now accompanied by the single command OBEY. The sticker campaign was eventually credited to the street artist Shepard Fairey, who'd created them with his schoolmates while a student at the Rhode Island School of Design. Fairey's famous now as a lawsuit-stricken imagery poacher, creator of the iconic Barack Obama CHANGE poster; he's as mediocre a poster boy for "appropriation aesthetics" as 2 Live Crew, whose sample of Roy Orbison's "Pretty Woman" thrust them into the Open Source vanguard, such as it was, in 1989. Fairey's stickers could be seen as a guerrilla-subliminal ad campaign for *They Live*, reinscribing the film's motif of icons of persuasion hidden in plain sight: our overlord's commands are visible if you know where to look. And we, the underground, make ourselves known to one another by outlawed modes: pirate broadcasts, signal jamming, samizdat pamphlets, graffiti. (Fairey's *They Live* reference also puns on Roddy Piper's career as a pro wrestler.)

They Live displays no fewer than four layers of public textual stuff. Three are under the filmmakers' control. First, the Matrix layer of manipulative fictions: the magazines, newspapers, and billboards for computers and vacations in the Caribbean. Second, the unmasked truth of obnoxious commands hidden beneath: OBEY, WATCH TV, HONOR APATHY, DOUBT HUMANITY, etcetera. Third, fake graffiti scrawls: THEY LIVE,

WE SLEEP. The fourth layer, imposed by the documentary effects of location shooting, and probably exaggerated by a budget prohibiting Antonioni-esque impulses to repaint the world, consists of whatever text was randomly immortalized in the camera's passing gaze: actual signage (like the freight train reading SHOCK CONTROL), or legitimately illegitimate graffiti (like the gnomic, concrete-poetic PARK CENT on the side of the Dumpster in Nada's alley).

Such accidental documentation isn't always negligible: my brother and other graffiti-artists-turned-graffiti-historians pore over those vintage New York City location films that contain subway scenes, like *The French Connection*, *Death Wish*, and *The Taking of Pelham, 1,2,3*, ferreting out lost traces of their subculture's origins. *They Live*'s special interest in fugitive modes of discourse isolates these random captures in a charged neutral zone. It's as if some third constituency, neither enchanted nor disenchanted by the alien broadcast, occupies the same city invisibly, and has sent SHOCK CONTROL and PARK CENT out as signs of their existence. Call this third constituency "the Real."

Fairey's interventions occupy the same uneasy middle ground as *They Live* itself: on the one hand, the termite arts of graffiti or of the deliberate B-movie, marginal activities carrying a subversive potential past the sentries of high art. On the other, the gallery-ready postures of text artists like Barbara Kruger and Jenny Holzer, or of the *Cahiers* table of "conscious" auteurs—Hitchcock being the supreme example—at which Carpenter may occasionally be granted a shaky seat.

Too poised and context-aware to be claimed as primitives, too crass and populist to be comfortably claimed for the high-art pantheon, Fairey and Carpenter both oscillate dismayingly in the void between.

Once, by chance, I attended a baseball game at San Francisco's Candlestick Park at which Jenny Holzer had been commissioned to "appropriate" the stadium's LED signs for her own artistic-subversive purposes. The vast and unfamiliar venue and audience was meant to exfoliate Holzer's art into the larger world. Being a Holzer fan, and learning of the planned intervention at the baseball game, I anticipated great things. My companion at the game knew nothing of Holzer's work, so I strained to set up his expectations. But the effort fizzled. When Holzer's enigmas crawled past on the signs, they died in the stadium's open-air light and the visual and auditory noise, baseball's common denominators. They'd become merely ineffectively opaque announcements, or advertisements for products we couldn't buy.

The discourse of commerce is a kind of quicker-picker-upper, superabsorbent of what happens along, even (or especially) that which presents itself as oppositional to, or critical of, commercial culture. So, much of Barbara Kruger's and Holzer's impact was gently naturalized within advertising language. This awkward  fact cuts against *They Live*'s central assertion: that the distance between the "lies" of commercial-ideological speech and the coercive "truths" smuggled inside it is an extreme one, and shattering to cross. Really, the two coexist and even mate with appalling ease (Recall the "ironic" generic packaging that was faddish in the eighties—cigarettes labeled CIGARETTES, and so on—that claimed to deny the sizzle of advertising allure in favor of the steak of gratified desire). Kruger and Holzer's non sequitur interventions briefly attained a gallant purity, but they'd always needed the gallery or museum context as a quarantine against recontamination. Their work degenerated anyway, refamiliarizing into po-mo moral rhetoric, or reappropriated for fashion layouts. What makes Shepard Fairey's populist gesture insipid is how self-evidently it awaited a product retrofit, a proceed-to-checkout button. When the OBEY T-shirt or CHANGE political campaign rolled out, no one, least of all the "artworks" themselves, even hiccupped.

Golf Magazine and Paperback Spinner-Rack

(34:02)

Delightful as is the translation of an entire newsstand's color-fully thin offerings into OBEY, CONSUME, SLEEP, etcetera, we may not bother to notice that the magazine framed longest for our consideration is a too-real *Golf Digest*, the cover of which shows a television set and the probably unsatirizable command, "Let T.V. Teach You!" (*They Live* thinks you've already done this.)

The spinner racks full of paperback books—equally too real to be fake—boast a squalid cross section of vicarious terror and wish fulfillment, tabloid opiate for the masses: Charles Berlitz's *Bermuda Triangle*, Darcy O'Brien's *Two of a Kind: The Hillside Stranglers*, Kevin J. Todeschi's *Edgar Cayce's ESP*. All three hint at worlds-within-the-world, promising to deliver an evil or transcendence lurking beyond unschooled sight. But honestly, *blech*. If I had an hour to kill, I'd stick to the magazines.

A Countenance

(34:32)

> As the night deepened, so deepened to me the interest of
> the scene; for not only did the general character of the crowd
> materially alter (its gentler features retiring in the gradual
> withdrawal of the more orderly portion of the people, and
> its harsher ones coming out into bolder relief, as the late
> hour brought forth every species of infamy from its den,)
> but the rays of the gas-lamps, feeble at first in their struggle
> with the dying day, had now at length gained ascendancy,
> and threw over every thing a fitful and garish lustre . . .
> With my brow to the glass, I was thus occupied in scru-
> tinizing the mob, when suddenly there came into view a
> countenance (that of a decrepit old man, some sixty-five or
> seventy years of age,)—a countenance which at once arrested
> and absorbed my whole attention, on account of the abso-
> lute idiosyncrasy of its expression.
>
> —Edgar Allan Poe, "The Man of the Crowd"

They're appalling, that's what they are. Walking disasters.
Flayed, scalded, piebald, grimacing, corrupted, robotic,
evoking syphilis-victim scare-photos from teenage health-ed
nightmares, yet somehow accusatory, defiant inside their disguises, the ghouls present no limit of affront to a healthy construction worker's eye. They look burnt, yet gooey. They're

also—how to say this?—affrontingly cheapo (eventually we'll even notice in their ghoul-hands what looks like the wrinkling of rubber dishwashing gloves, and so this may be another reason for the black-and-white: better to mask low-budget inadequacies). This fact frees a certain relieving hilarity, yet also synthesizes with our revulsion: Something this skeezy is ruling my world? Something this ludicrous is freaking me out? (The virtuosity of Carpenter's mise-en-scène ensures it is.) The first to turn to the camera and say, more or less, *'Fuck you lookin' at?'* is this silver-haired, foxy older gentleman of obvious privilege referred to in the credits as "Well-Dressed Customer"; his sustained, withering ghoul-glare as he purchases his magazine (with dollars that confess THIS IS YOUR GOD) is one of *They Live*'s icons, an instant that punches a spooky hole in time. Nada hasn't located his voice yet, so we're left undistracted, or unconsoled, by any cheese-dip-Brazilian-plastic-surgery-perfume-on-a-pig one-liners. What's brilliantly guaranteed is how totally we'd loathe this guy *anyway*; you may not be going home in your BMW and Rolex to soak in your Jacuzzi, but he certainly is. So, already brewing within our terror is a lavish contempt, one that finds satisfaction at the rotten-corpse visage before us. Any rich guy who's ever glowered at us like we didn't belong somewhere—an outdoor magazine rack, for chrissakes!—really ought to look as sick on the outside as we're certain he is in his soul. *I'm fucking looking at* you, *man!* Nada's not quite there, but he's just a step away.

Also, ghouls wear wigs. For some reason their masterful illusion-generator can't do hair. Don't think about this too hard.

News Vendor

(35:27)

How race-conscious is *They Live*? We've met six black men in the film up to this point: the mute pedestrian hypnotized by the television montage; the blind preacher ("It's the revolution!"); the construction worker Frank ("Leave it alone, man!"); the unnamed church conspirator, who isn't given any lines; (the drugged-out squatter ("Welcome to the party"); and the news vendor ("I don't want no hassle today"). They're seers or non-seers, specifically (Frank will be given the privilege of changing from the latter to the former). No black man will ever be uncovered as a ghoul.

Code and Canon

"Give me a line from some literary work," Prandtl said, turning to me.

"Shakespeare?"

"Whatever you like."

"You maintain that his plays are nothing but coded messages?"

"Depends what you mean by a coded message. But let's give it a try, shall we?"

I tried to think, but nothing came to me except Othello's "Excellent Wretch!" That seemed a bit brief and inappropriate.

"I've got it!" I announced with sudden inspiration. 'My ears have not yet drunk a hundred words of that tongue's utterance, yet I know the sound: Art thou not Romeo and a Montague?'

"Fine."

Prandtl had hardly typed this out when the tape began to move from the slot, a paper snake. He gently handed the end of it to me, and I waited patiently while the printout emerged. The vibration of the machine suddenly stopped and the rest of the tape came out blank. I read:

"BAS TARD MATT HEWS VAR LET MATT HEWS SCUM WOULD BASH THAT FLAP EAR ASS WITH PLEA SURE GREAT THAT MATT HEWS BAS"

"What's this?" I asked, perplexed. Prandtl gave a knowing nod.

"Shakespeare evidently harbored a grudge against someone by the name of Matthews and chose to put this in code when he wrote those lines."

"What? You mean he deliberately used that beautiful scene to disguise a lot of foul language directed at some Matthews?"

"Who says he did it deliberately? A code is a code, regardless of the author's intention."

"Let's see something," I said, and typed the decoded text into the machine myself. The tape moved again, spiraling onto the floor. Prandtl smiled but said nothing.

"IF ONLY SHE'D GIVE ME TRA LA LA LA TRA LA LA LA IF ONLY TRA LA LA SHE'D GIVE ME LA LA, TRA LA LA AND GIVE ME TRA LA LA HA HA HA TRA LA LA" went the letters of the printout.

"Now what do you make of it?"

"We have moved deeper into the seventeenth-century Englishman's psyche."

—Stanislaw Lem, *Memoirs Found in a Bathtub*

This tale of a lonely wanderer has become a narrative of *interpretation* (one that both begs and systematically deranges the interpretive impulse, like mine in this book). The world of the film, while still "analog," nevertheless possesses a source code: *They Live* is *The Matrix* for an era of fax machines and fisticuffs. As many will have discovered in college English seminars, subjecting a given text to such scorched-earth interpretive vigor as the Hoffman lenses have brought to these billboards and magazines is to debunk the mystique of textual authority per se—and frequently to smuggle in an anti-historical, canon-smashing glee, not precisely what the professor intended. From a sophomoric perspective, if this stuff's all just *symbols*, why bother? We don't need no education / we don't need no thought control. If language is a virus, take a cure.

Ghoul Motivation

> Look at the front pages of our daily newspapers. Every title, especially when it pretends just to inform us, contains an implicit injunction. So when you are asked to choose between liberal democracy and fundamentalism, it is not only that one term is obviously preferred; what is more important, the true injunction is to see this as the true choice, to ignore third options. So, again, naïve as it may seem, the film's staging of ideology is nonetheless more complex than it may appear. Once you put the glasses on and see it, it no longer determines you. Which means that before you see it through the glasses, you also saw it, but you were not aware of it.
>
> —Slavoj Žižek, "They Live!
> Hollywood as an Ideological Machine"

What's odd in retrospect about the ghoul at the newsstand is that *he wants to read the newspapers*. This appears to be far more than a show of interest on his part; he even takes one home, pausing to scowl at some headline before getting into his car. Similarly, the ghoul at the bar at the end of the film sits watching television, as absorbed as any of the other patrons. How can we account for this? Which do the ghouls' robotic orbs register as they scan (presumably like a supermarket laser run over a bar code) the dummy media with which they've overpainted our world: exhortations like CONFORM and OBEY, or the illusory articles and photographs, or both?

Maybe they're seeing some third-level media, something we'd have to call "Real Ghoul News," which is being broadcast on a wavelength perceptible only to their eyes. Huh. I wish I could say the film's given me some help here, but I'm flying solo.

But this, another of *They Live*'s zones of lively incoherence, really raises the matter of ghoul motivation in general terms. Throw out my third-level-media theory: it's likely the ghoul cares about the delusional broadcast that rules the human world because of his investment in the mass-consensual fiction that has resulted (at both levels of the word *investment*). After all, these entities have troubled to turn up here on Earth, to seek out hard-to-maintain bespoke suits and clumpy wigs, to tool around in our fancier cars when they could simply teleport, and to shop for blue-corn tortillas—in most regards they've bought the same ticket they're selling. So, this gentleman's probably checking his stock prices (even with the fix in, you can never be too sure the ghoul down the street isn't getting ahead of you), but also perusing the Real Estate and Fashion sections, and Arts too, to see what recordings the hip ghouls are listening to these days. Maybe he's a sports fan, too. The only part of the paper surely of no interest whatsoever would be the news per se—whether international or domestic, all such conflicts would seem to be tempests in teapots now, bogus distractions definitively trumped by the larger fact of alien invasion and control. Finally, it might just be that buying a newspaper to read while stopped at red lights helps this succubus feel important and real. The way he wants to feel. Human.

Tracing the film's outward logic—"we're livestock!"—suggests the ghouls are something along the lines of farmers who want to dress up as cows. At the very least, they're like borderline cool kids in high school, just trying to fit in, to get over.

Stunned Maid

(36:25)

An unpleasantly gossiping female ghoul ("she didn't even go to Lamaze class") loads the spoils of a shopping spree into her car's open hatchback, talking the ear off a beleaguered older woman—her mother-in-law? Or a housekeeper?— who seemingly is the packhorse on this expedition. At the frame's right edge stands a young Latina dressed in the frilly costume of a Douglas Sirk-era maid. The expression on her face is of nearly lobotomized desensitization, as though she'd been hired that very morning, immediately stuffed into the absurd outfit, and now can't quite believe the future she sees stretching before her.

In a film that shows little interest in Hispanic Los Ange-les (the sort-of-exception being the mass of indolent, jocular unionized construction workers) and that, by calling its ex-traplanetary invaders "ghouls," seems to have gone out of its way *not* to explore any "illegal alien" resonances in its central motif (for contrast, consider 2009's *District 9*, or *They Live*'s 1988 contemporary *Alien Nation*), this stunned Chicana maid leaps out as one of the film's piercing details—that is, if you spot her at all. She's so far to the side that anything short of full-aspect-ratio crops her out entirely. Carpenter is a famous exponent of wide-screen composition, not ordinarily considered a stance with political implications. Here, though, the Panavision broadens social context: at the periphery of a scene, "the help" becomes visible. What's more, the commitment to the use of the screen's far edges aligns with *They Live*'s attack on television, as impoverished in its aesthetics as it is impoverishing otherwise.

In my "perfect sequence," right after the maid might be the place (six and a half minutes in) to quit. Or then again, not.

Grocery Store

(36:40)

Wobbling, perhaps showing signs of truth-drunkenness or truth-migraine, Nada staggers through the doorway of a grocery store—an upscale one, presumably, and seething with ghouls, though the store's old-fashioned aisles, with displays low enough to look and speak across, may remind film buffs of the site of Fred MacMurray's and Barbara Stanwyck's nerve-wracked assignations in *Double Indemnity*. In here, Nada will break the lush spell of the long sequence by, at last, opening his mouth, and beginning to bellow out his signature lead-balloon quips. He'll also, as an immediate result, get busted by a particularly repugnant, fur-wearing old-lady ghoul, who hisses into her wristwatch-communicator, "I've got one that can *see*!" From that moment on Nada's a hunted man, and one bent on, or at least bending toward, vengeance.

First, though, after wandering through the food aisles and taking the measure of an assorted tableau of yuppie-ghoul snarkiness (one cackles at a friend's having served blue-corn tortillas—"so dated"; another irritably dismisses the career anxieties of an overtly depressed human colleague), Nada meets another television set, the first since Justiceville. On the screen, a Reaganite politician blathers about "Morning in America" in front of a gigantic OBEY banner. For an instant this broadcast reverses like a photographic negative, accompanied by a feedback-like whine in the (fairly subliminal here) musical score. Either the hackers are trying to break through again, or this represents an instant of expressionistic emphasis from the director, as the film steps out and names its political targets, a suspicion perhaps confirmed by Nada's response. The befuddled adventurer seems to relax into his disgust at the inevitability of it all and, chuckling, finds his tongue at last: "It *figures* it'd be something like *this*." (Another place my perfect sequence could quit—here.)

The spectacle of so many ghouls placidly testing the ripeness of citrus and gathering up frozen dinners calls up recollection of William S. Burroughs's simple explanation of the title of *Naked Lunch*: "A frozen moment when everyone sees what is on the end of every fork." Certainly, *They Live* has come out of hiding.

Into the Cheese Dip

(38:01)

Out of hiding, the film then dives into what's impossible not to call "the cheese dip." Nada, enraged at all he's begun to understand, unstoppers what will become a tirade of insults against (almost exclusively female) ghouls for their revolting appearance: "You look like your head fell in the cheese dip back in 1957." This is probably the time to address the question of how committed *They Live* is to its sporadic misogyny—after Well-Dressed Customer at the newsstand, we've basked in Nada's disgust at female ghouls under beauty-shop hairdryers, female ghouls gossiping and shopping, and now this aging, "real fucking ugly" female ghoul in furs. Just outside the grocery store he'll pause to denounce a female ghoul primping at her reflection in a shop window: "That's like putting perfume on a pig!" Coming soon, one of the movie's nonstarter rallying cries: "Life's a bitch and she's back in heat!"

Is *They Live* coming unglued, tipping a hand we didn't want to know it was holding? Or are these reasonable insights into Nada's sense of the world and his place in it? Let's acknowledge, at least, that this man of the people is more of the male than of the female people. And that if we've blundered into a director's blind spot, fellow leftist iconoclasts of John Carpenter's vintage (1946) more than offer him company there.

Anyway, my perfect sequence is over by the time Nada stumbles out of the grocery store, probably sometime before.

Is Nada the Stupidest Person in the Movie?

> Taught to love Brando from the beginning, we can no longer
> criticize him at any particular moment or even acknowledge
> his objective stupidity . . . We can sum up Kazan's mistake
> by saying that what should have been judged was much less
> the capitalist than Brando himself. For there is much more
> to expect from the rebellion of victims than from the carica-
> ture of their masters.
>
> —Roland Barthes, discussing *On the Waterfront*,
> in "A Sympathetic Worker"

If paranoia generally turns its sufferers into cartoons—even,
sadly, the righteous paranoia of the just-because-you're-
paranoid-doesn't-mean-they-aren't-after-you variety—the
particular cartoon Nada turns into is Yosemite Sam. Up to
this point, Nada's self-protective instincts, at least, haven't
been half bad. He's muscled and squinted his way into our
hearts. Yet from here on his sputtering, red-faced imprudence
verges on the cretinous. Maybe that's been the point all
along: to subject a pure unthinking lumpenprole (Who else
would have gazed at L.A.'s skyline and said, "I believe in
America"?) to an allegory so blatant that *even he* can see the
truth about capitalism.

Bifurcation

> What Hitchcock does, in effect, for the first half of the film, he gives you an extraordinary sort of modern novel, and he then gives you a slasher film.
>
> —David Thomson

The question, then, is how far will Nada drag the film with him? The art film is over, that's for certain. The action movie is underway.

This matter of *They Live*'s bifurcation can be taken one of two ways. Is it a case like *Psycho*, a film that builds in tension toward an incomparable shock in its first forty minutes, then, unable to match what's been delivered, flattens into a routine whodunnit? (This view, typified by David Thomson's *The Moment of Psycho*, does Hitchcock's monument some injustice, but it floats out there). Or are we seeing instead a Kubrickian strategy of halves, like that in *Full Metal Jacket*: first a thesis in desensitization, then an indignant exhibition of its costs? (Other Kubrick films might be seen as subtler precursors for this split strategy: *Barry Lyndon*, *The Shining*.) Or is it something between the two? Am I hedging here? Sure I am!

We Have Met the Enemy and He Is Not Us

(39:30)

"You're not understanding, are you? You're refusing to deal with what I'm telling you. The brain does the thinking. The meat."

"Thinking meat! You're asking me to believe in thinking meat!"

"Yes, thinking meat! Conscious meat! Loving meat. Dreaming meat. The meat is the whole deal! Are you beginning to get the picture or do I have to start all over?"

"Omigod. You're serious, then. They're made out of meat."

"Thank you. Finally. Yes. They are indeed made out of meat. And they've been trying to get in touch with us for almost a hundred of their years."

"Omigod. So what does this meat have in mind?"

"First it wants to talk to us. Then I imagine it wants to explore the Universe, contact other sentiences, swap ideas and information. The usual."

"We're supposed to talk to meat."

—Terry Bisson, "They're Made out of Meat"

The plot hinges right here: to kill a cop is to relegate yourself to outlaw status in any system, on Alpha Centauri as on Earth. Nada kills two, then raids their cruiser for weaponry.

The Hays Code may no longer prevail under present circumstances, but this is looking more and more like a Sam Peckinpah film (an echo confirmed by the score, which provides a martial drumbeat derived from *The Wild Bunch* as Nada pump-loads his shotgun). Even Kris "Rubber Duck" Kristofferson in *Convoy* wasn't fated to survive his anti-authoritarian stand; Nada's prospects for macho martyrdom have begun to heave into view.

Was there another way to play it? The cop suggests they "go someplace quiet and talk this over"; is Nada a prospective recruit for the human power elite? Hard to be sure. Anyway, Nada doesn't linger over the possibility. He's still too freaking enraged by their cheese-dip faces. "You look as shitty to us as we do to you," bluffs the cop, but Nada swats it away: "Impossible."

This, in its way, is a key exchange. We intuitively ratify Nada's scorn at what would ordinarily seem a traditional science-fiction platitude, with its overtones of a Franz Boas cultural relativism: Why shouldn't we at least *try* to accept the creatures' validity on their own terms, and believe that they might be attractive or sympathetic, at the very least, to one another? (cf. *Enemy Mine* [1985], in which Lou Gossett, Jr., laboriously redeems the reptilian foulness of his facial prosthetics). But no. Nothing could rehabilitate the withered deathmasks these ghouls bear through life, and they're obviously yearning both to resemble and to, er, *mingle* with our smooth, unblotched selves (a suspicion endorsed in a big way in the film's last scene). We may Sleep while They Live, but They also Suck, and We Rock.

By the eighties, "deep" sci-fi or horror, like Ridley Scott's *Blade Runner* (1982) or David Cronenberg's *The Fly* (1986), was meant to enmesh our sympathies in some complicated revision of our definition of "the human," but in *They Live* John Carpenter isn't having any of it. He's put his 1950s monster-movie foot down: these are Pod People, people! *Wake up!* Creatures walk among us, monsters from the yuppie id. No director's cut is due to emerge wherein Nada's subtly revealed as a ghoul himself, one programmed to believe himself human, and poignantly enlisted to hunt down and slaughter his own kind. "I've seen things you people wouldn't believe . . . a blue-corn tortilla on fire off the shoulder of Orion . . ."

Still, Nada never *does* wear his Hoffman lenses for a look in the mirror.

Quip in a Bank

(41:04)

> I've come here to chew bubblegum and kick ass. And I'm all
> out of ass.   —*Mystery Science Theater 3000*

> I have been programmed to eviscerate your repulsive squishy
> organic bits and chew gum. And I hate gum.
>   —*Marvel Zombies 3*

> I have come from the frozen heart of Naxxramas to feast on
> souls and deliver a vicious thrashing upon our sworn en-
> emies. And I'm all out of souls.   —*World of Warcraft*

Nada walks (backward) into a bank, there to take measure of
yet another tableau of ghoul penetration of the daily life of the
marketplace. Then he squares himself and his weaponry, in
the manner of William Holden and his colleagues bracing for
their suicidal fuck-you slaughter in *The Wild Bunch*. Only, in
place of the weary determination of Holden's "Let's go," Nada
delivers an ostentatious quip with a admirable lack of ostenta-
tion (Piper is anchored in his WWF comfort zone here, selling what's rococo as working-class grit), though in principle
the quip extends the air of blustery self-amusement begun in
the market's cheese-dip aisle. Some accounts credit the quip
as a Piper improvisation: "I've come here to chew bubblegum
and kick ass. And I'm all out of bubblegum."

The line has a vibrant posthumous life, recursing through a video game called Duke Nukem and detaching from there into the popular unconscious. The unexplored subtext is, again, cloddish stupidity, as when Gerald Ford was mocked by the Chevy Chases of the world for being unable to "chew gum and walk at the same time." Unlike a Republican president, Nada can do both, as the quip implicitly brags. That's if he could afford to chew gum, or would actually bother to do so—chewing gum being the opposite of nourishment, a kind of newsstand magazine or television program for the tongue and teeth. You're not allowed to buy gum with food stamps, but then, as was established earlier, Nada's type of person is out of food stamps, too. Not ammunition, though.

Amiri Baraka: "If you play James Brown (say, 'Money Won't Change You . . . but time will take you out') in a bank, the total environment is changed . . . An energy is released in the bank, a summoning of images that take the bank, and everybody in it, on a trip. That is, they visit another place. A place where Black People live." *They Live*'s bank is a high-vaulted, echoey stone palace, still common enough in 1988, but dwindling since, as major-city chains like Chase and Wells Fargo abandon the (literal) high overhead and overt architectural power dynamics of such real estate commitments and disperse instead into myriad shallow storefronts: bank as Dunkin' Donuts. Future viewers may register the pointless grandeur of such interiors as this one with puzzlement.

Or not. After all, their resonance will have survived in movie iconography. From Capra's *American Madness* through hundreds of Westerns and gangster films, to *It's a Wonderful*

Life, *Bonnie and Clyde*, *Dog Day Afternoon*, *Inside Man*, and, yes, *The Wild Bunch*, the entry of an existentially kinetic (and usually armed) man or group of men into one of money's static and forbidding palaces forms a basic Hollywood enactment of the anxiety of individual fate and imperative when confronted with the slablike facts—the twenty-four-inch vault doors, the gated windows—of power, access, class, and privilege. In the myth, the individual makes off at least temporarily with the loot, though from that point he's a wanted man, his clock ticking. To triumph rather than be pulled back to earth, an escape across some border is probably indicated. (*They Live* has already cited this archetype twice. Gilbert, in the fake church, expresses his exasperation with the resistance movement's present strategies: "robbing banks, manufacturing Hoffman lenses 'til we're blue in the face." And Drifter, cynically retailing rumors of far-off rebellion, mentions "shootin' people, robbin' banks, same old thing as always.")

Nada's situation on entering the bank, though, is atypical—having just killed a cop, he's already crossed the line, made his outlaw commitment. Anyway, he's wearing the glasses; this bank's legible, and unintimidating. The majestic vintage marble column and gilded steelwork interior has been dragged into the prosaic contemporary by some shoddy renovation as well as by the presence of new signage, readily translated: OBEY, WATCH TV, DO NOT QUESTION AUTHORITY, and so on. If money declares "I am your God," then Nada's here to defile a church (and never in moviedom has an armed intruder showed less interest in a bank's loot). If he's worked it out in advance—more likely, we feel, he's working on instinct—

Nada would have to hope to cross some particularly remote border, one separating him in time or space from all he's just learned about his world, to melt back into any crowd. By delivering his quip, he declares his lack of interest in remaining civilian, the decision that will define his actions for the remainder of the film. No one threatens Nada here; he starts the trouble. The bank becomes an arena for testing a new policy of taking out as many ghouls as he can, while sparing the deluded (and, presumably, often complicit) humans.

My own bank branch as of this writing, on Montague Street in Brooklyn Heights, happens to resemble Nada's (though it's undoubtedly older): a looming marble palace rendered mundane by crappy renovation and generic corporate furnishings. The public language inside this space is contradictorily "double," like the public language in *They Live*. On the one hand, carved deep in burnished stone, high above our heads and the grand interior lintels, are two mottos. The first: COMMERCE DEFIES EVERY WIND, OUTRIDES EVERY TEMPEST, AND INVADES EVERY ZONE. (Google reveals these to be the words of the historian George Bancroft. They're also etched above the entrance to the Department of Commerce in Washington, D.C.) The second: SOCIETY IS BUILT UPON TRUST, AND TRUST UPON CONFIDENCE IN ONE ANOTHER'S INTEGRITY. (Google: Robert South, seventeen-century English poet.) Meanwhile, blaring from cardboard and vinyl signs as well as a video screen placed behind the teller's heads, the following messages: POCKET A LITTLE PIXIE DUST! DISNEY-REWARDS DEBIT CARD FROM CHASE, GIVING YOU THE MOST MAGICAL OF PERKS AND THE DREAMIEST OF

REWARDS. YOUR EVERYDAY MAGIC! Another: A WINNER EVERY FIVE MINUTES: CHASE PICKS UP THE TAB IS BACK! And the fuzzily Orwellian MORE REWARDS ON CHASE FREEDOM. No Hoffman lenses are required to contemplate the weird gulf, the incoherent void that looms between these two versions of civic discourse, which offer themselves as some kind of tragic microcosm of Tocqueville's *Democracy in America*—or an allegory of Ralph Waldo Emerson dragged bodily into a Disney casino. No one in my bank remarks on this, or gives evidence of seeing. Though we're all wearing the glasses here, we seem to find ourselves blinded—or rendered dumb—by what they reveal.

Not a Cop-Hater as Such

(42:28)

A twee hovering surveillance device confronts Nada in the bank's alley. Nada destroys it with his shotgun; when it explodes, he covers his head with his arms to shelter himself from flying fragments someone apparently forgot to bring to the set that morning. Fire the continuity girl! Then a single human cop arrives, to be easily disarmed and chased off: the cop is bald and mild (Nada doesn't even really need Hoffman lenses here, since we know ghouls can afford wigs!) and Nada's pumped up with rage, his hormones and mane flowing. A brief, forgettable exchange, but we're learning things: not all cops are ghouls, and Nada is capable, in his fury, of making these important distinctions. I'd venture, though it's impossible to prove, that given this cop's bewildered reactions he's no member of the human power elite, but a dupe, innocent of the conspiracy.

Since rank-and-file policemen and soldiers are usually manipulatable like this fellow—trained into unquestioning obeisance to command—why so many ghoul policemen and bank guards and SWAT teams? The pragmatic answer: Nada needs armed troops to engage with and murder. Too many civilian ghoul kills might look unsporting. But it suggests that ghouls brought with them their own hierarchies, even as they imposed themselves generally as our overlords. Do those who came all this way only to have to drive around in police cars resent those who get to play politicians on television?

Thirty-Nine Steps

(43:11)

Holly, played by Meg Foster, enters story and frame in an explicitly Hitchcockian shot, derived from the opening of *Marnie* particularly: walking away from a worm's-eye view, our sense of receding perspective enhanced by her framing in the center of the pillar-and-beam architecture of a parking garage. A neat pale-gray purse and matching heels, plus Foster's hypnotically smooth stride, complete the reference.

Nada's lurking in the garage. Improvising a plan to convey himself out of the bank's vicinity, he'll carjack Holly, making her the last arriving of the film's major characters. Here, *They Live* slows, to give the two a chance to make their pensive, peculiar connection—a truth-sinking-in interlude for both Nada and the viewer—and to tempt us briefly with notions of solace, exchanged confidences, even romance. But it's to be a wrong number, in the end.

There's a tenacious movie archetype afoot in this next six minutes of film: the persecuted (usually wrongly accused) man who attaches himself to or absconds with an unwilling female, who then finds herself challenged to evaluate his protestations of innocence, and/or the credibility of the paranoiac plot he claims to be the target of. The point of origin is probably *The 39 Steps* (1935); if some earlier denominator exists, credit for conveyance of this narrative gesture into the filmgoer's imaginative stockpile surely goes to Hitchcock anyway, and he reuses it, with variations, in *Young and Innocent*, *Saboteur*, and *North by Northwest*. (Even *Rear Window* has an element of paranoid-guy-pleads-his-case.)

The gesture often involves some negotiation of class difference, or simply a taming-of-the-shrew toppling of the heroine's snobbish reserve toward a frantic Everyman. The great example, outside Hitchcock, is the Robert Redford-Faye Dunaway relationship in Sydney Pollack's *Three Days of the Condor* (1975); Pollack deftly shifts the film's subjectivity toward Dunaway's character, letting us feel the threat of

Redford's invasion of her sanctuary even as we're rooting for him to persuade her of his story. Nada's kidnapping of Holly feels like a compressed low-budget retread or even satire of *Condor*, due partly to the poor man's Dunaway of Meg Foster's sultry-bordering-on-somnolent performance: you're no Redford, Piper, and, no, you're not getting any! The versatile *39 Steps* motif found its nadir in Richard Donner's punishingly literal *Conspiracy Theory* (1997), where the distance between Mel Gibson's justified paranoiac (complete with stalker behavior and black government helicopters) and the harassed patience of Julia Roberts proves to be a bridge not worth crossing. Something like blowing up into the sly next minutes of *They Live* into a glib and shrill full-length feature.

Porn Again

This is the first time we've seen Roddy Piper cross the threshold of a middle-class interior. It retriggers alarms. Everybody knows what happens when the actors dressed as construction workers come indoors in Southern California. Holly says, "I'll do what you tell me"; she also falls to her knees at Nada's crotch when, pulling her into her living room, he first stumbles to the floor. Really, I'm not making this up: the phallic cactus and vaginal sculpture, the white-leather couch, most of all Holly's pot-smoking, open-shirted gay neighbors, who arch their eyebrows and purse their lips as they watch their ice-queen neighbor apparently answering a midday booty call: all these indicate, and *you* know, what happens when the actors dressed as construction workers come indoors in Southern California. So does John Carpenter, who in his early seventies apprenticeship dashed off several porn-film scripts. The point I want to emphasize is this: Carpenter really doesn't care whether or not you get that he gets it. He'd far sooner be mistaken for an audience-laughing-at-you-not-with-you artist than slow the pace of his film, or wreck its tone, by underlining the jokes.

The Puzzle of Holly

Holly owns a car, and lives (apparently by herself) in a house on the hill. As Thom Andersen showed in *Los Angeles Plays Itself*, such homes traditionally are implicated with villainy. She works at Cable 54—probably a bad sign if we think it through. She's gorgeous and eerie and some viewers find her irritatingly detached (others find her mannish, apparently: Meg Foster was nominated for a "Meanie Award" for "Most Mannish Features by a Woman in a Roddy Piper Film"). She played Hester Prynne (probably not significant), and in Sam Peckinpah's last film, *The Osterman Weekend* (more likely significant). She'll betray our hero like a femme fatale, but the noir actress she's "doing" seems to be Lauren Bacall, who's always sympathetic; these mixed signifiers keep her interesting. Her eyes are such a pale shade of blue they're nearly a special effect—read, "zombie," or a forecast of Carpenter's remake of *Village of the Damned*. Roddy Piper, his talent having matured in the pro wrestling arena, never gets a grip on how to play opposite a female and/or such a contained performer (he's also just not that good at creating many variations on "acting woozy"); in comparison to her understatement, he seems now to be pitching everything at the back row.

Holly's place in the story twists, twice. The first twist, when she reappears in the revolutionary cell, most viewers find coherent, and satisfying (partly because it rekindles a flicker of romance for poor Nada). The second, when she betrays Nada to the ghouls, is obscure, and forces the viewer to work backward to this first long scene, wondering where her sympathies lie at the start. The three alternatives are like a braid: either she learns of the conspiracy after his visit, joins the underground, and is subsequently corrupted into ghoul alliance in time to betray Nada; or she learns of the conspiracy and is immediately corrupted and joins the underground as a mole; or she's been corrupted the whole time and manipulates Nada with her bogus passivity throughout. (If she's a long-time member of the human power elite, you've got to admire Holly's cool—but really, no matter what conclusion you reach, you've got to admire her cool.) What might seem the principle clue—her phone call to the cops after she's clobbered Nada through her picture window, down into the ravine—parses no matter what your interpretation (a genuine innocent would call what she believed were genuine police; a human traitor would ring the ghoul cops). Another clue—the shot establishing that Nada has left his Hoffman lenses behind on Holly's carpet—is equally versatile. We're finally left to draw our own conclusions in this matter, a radical piece of indeterminacy in such a forthright narrative machine.

One Great Shot

(49:57)

> Logically, there's every reason why this formal effect should have multiple "motivations." Nothing is imposed by some code or convention which would *demand* such a shot; it's Hitchcock's free, optional, and unique assemblage, and it's bio-ergonomic (it gears in with spectators' visual perceptions). The "overhead viewpoint" has no specific meaning. Sometimes it distances us from the action, or depersonalizes it, or grants us God-like objectivity: here, the disorientation is highly *lyrical*; and though it "makes strange," Brechtian alienation it sure ain't.
>
> —Raymond Durgnat, "Seven Reasons for One Great Shot,"
> in *A Long Hard Look at "Psycho"*

The breathtaking, close-overhead shot as Holly smashes the wine bottle over Nada's head, then leverages his bulk through a plate of glass and out of her life, owes plenty to the legendary close-overhead from *Psycho*, where Norman-Mother closes on the detective Arbogast at the top of the Bates-house stairs, assaulting him simultaneously with a knife blade and with gravity. In both shots the victim is hacked about the head, then plummets.

Carpenter's choice might seem ostentatious, but we're forced to respect its startling efficiency as an assault on our

nerves—and this functions metonymically for the startling efficiency of Holly's assault on Nada. Like a hostess keeping wineglasses topped without anyone noticing she's even pouring, Holly uses her right hand to sweep the bottle from its place and, with it, brain Nada, then replaces the bottle as she completes her turn. Meanwhile, her own glass remains serenely cradled in her left arm's fingers, even as her left elbow is used to judo him through the window. If this were a cocktail party, Holly would now resume small talk. Everything in this staging serves to destabilize our sense of a reliable and comprehensible physical environment. Even before the violence begins, the shot creates a spatial rupture: we had no idea, from the earlier shot-countershot, that the couch and the window, or Nada and Holly, were as near to each other as the overhead reveals them to be. Since control of his own (apparently dominant) physicality is all Nada's got—we've reveled at his ability to mow down ghoul cops and evade capture—the costs here, to the viewer's vicarious powers, are immense.

Holly, introduced with a Hitchcockian shot, now goes out with one (her sudden and bracing act of self-defense may also recall Grace Kelly getting ahold of the scissors in *Dial M for Murder*.) Raymond Durgnat suggests that what *Psycho*'s overhead shot conceals (without making it obvious that anything's being concealed) is Norman-Mother's face. The same shot in *They Live* cloaks Holly's expression as she demolishes our strongman. Yet would seeing what played over her features at that instant have given away Holly's affiliation? Given the serenity of her phone call immediately following, I doubt it.

Vertical City Inhospitable to
Horizontal Man

(50:06)

Nada had once strolled into the flat part of Los Angeles, con-
fident in what he had to offer, carrying his own tools. Now
he tumbles, slips, staggers and scrabbles and slides down the
hilly part, bruised and groaning, with nothing but the torn
clothes on his back, deprived of even his cheap sunglasses.

Who says this isn't still a Western in some part of its soul?

The alley where Nada spends the night is little better than
a shaft of light, occupying a mere third of the screen. Helicopter *thwacka-thwacka* overhead. *Bum-bum-bum, Waaah-wah!*

Jump Back in the Alley

(52:19)

The morning after, Nada walks the same overpass as he did in the rainy, main-title sequence, albeit now he's limping. Together with a return to the construction site, this cues the notion of a "reset" for the film, and for our anonymous man-of-the-streets. But Nada can't really get back there, a fact made clear in Frank's panicked reactions to the newly minted cop-killer, like the sighting of an apparition in daylight. Refused, Nada reenters downtown (there's the Los Angeles Athletic Club again), and then his alley, where he's stashed the carton of Hoffman lenses in a trashcan. The low-budget recycling of the same few backdrops—overpass, construction site, Athletic Club sidewalk, alley—lends the film a theatrical-allegorical quality, like a Beckett play, or a Budd Boetticher Western where the cowboys keep riding past the same few scenic geological outcroppings.

On the street before he reaches the alley, Nada hustles nervously past the shop window featuring the rows of televisions, now displaying a news bulletin featuring a (black-and-white!) photograph of Nada himself, a piece of superefficient shorthand for the common film noir motif of the city-wide, all-points-bulletin manhunt. The photo on the screen, rather than being, say, a blown-up still from the bank's surveillance cameras, depicts Nada with a shorter haircut and a distinctly relaxed, unhaunted expression. This is a glimpse of happier days (in Denver?), a throb of implied backstory for this itinerant Nothingman.

Garbage Truck

(53:45)

The glasses are gone. The trashcan is empty. The garbage truck is leaving the alley. The glasses are in the garbage truck!

Pointless practical obstructions, logistical detours, MacGuffin-withholdings, et al.—these exasperate and delight us by forcing us to grant our susceptibility to the director's whims. After Fred MacMurray's stalled car starts again in *Double Indemnity*, or Robert Walker succeeds in fishing the lighter out of the grate in *Strangers on a Train*, and we can breathe again, and the "real" plot resumes, we're reconfirmed in our investment in the film's stakes. That we cared that Nada's glasses were gone shows we've collaborated in constructing their imaginary power. To question the garbage truck interlude would be to plant a first step on a slippery slope, that of unmaking our fundamental bargain with narrative. We've got no choice but to climb in there with him and scrabble for the precious $2.99 prop.

Plunging a Yojimbo-like hero into the shit, the murk of life, is also a traditional ritual, a passage that proves his legitimate commonality, his humble worthiness as the righteous, return-of-the-repressed opposition to power's repressive force (cf. the Death Star trash-compactor sequence in *Star Wars*). The only problem is that this truck's not full of organic matter, but confetti, like the stuff you'd toss from a Wall Street window at the Yankees. Watching, my friend Laura shrieked with delight: "They couldn't afford real garbage!"

Fight, Fight

(55:23)

[I]t's a very strange fight—there are moments of exchanges of friendly smiles, and it's in itself totally irrational. Why doesn't [Frank] put the glasses on, just to satisfy his friend? The one explanation is that he knows that his friend wants him to see something dangerous, to attain a prohibited knowledge which would totally spoil the relative peace of his daily life. The violence staged here, this violence of the two of them fighting, is a positive violence, a condition of liberation. The lesson is that our liberation from ideology is not a spontaneous act, an act of discovering our true self. And that's what I find convincing in this simple scene . . . just think how it totally turns around the usual new age idea of critique of ideology, which would be: "in everyday life we have ideological glasses, learn to put down, take off, the glasses, and see with your own eyes reality the way it is." No, unfortunately, it doesn't work like this. Liberation hurts. You have to be forced to put your glasses on.

—Slavoj Žižek, "They Live!
Hollywood as an Ideological Machine"

A fabulous movie (except for that endless fight behind the building).   —Greil Marcus

"The actual fight, when they're in the back lot, and they're fighting, was, uh, the fight sequence from, what's that movie, *They Live*? So, uh, we took that fight sequence where, damn, what's the wrestler's name? Roddy Rowdy Piper? And that other dude, that black dude, they have this knock-down, drag-out fight in this alley in *They Live* . . . We actually animated to that soundtrack, so, for a while, before we put our own sounds in it, it was, like, Jimmy and Timmy fighting, but it was the sounds, the grunts from Roddy Piper, from *They Live*, with the music and all that . . . It was actually pretty funny that way, and I think it ended up on the Internet that way or something . . . The original version . . . it's a great fight sequence in *They Live* . . . *They Live* is a . . could have been a . . . it's a pretty great movie, uh . . ."

—Trey Parker and Matt Stone,
commentary track for *South Park* "Cripple Fight" episode

How to legislate between these great constituencies: those who love *They Live* for the fight scene, and those who love it despite the fight scene? Indefensible by its deep design, the "longest fight scene in movie history" (according to Carpenter, who has also claimed that Roddy Piper and Keith David rehearsed it for three weeks) expands in cultural memory as an artifact unto itself, an object if not of study then of wonder, a legend, a contested site, a nihilistic gesture, a secret code or ritual, possibly akin to Fight Club before *Fight Club*. Yet for all its uses as a screen for fannish or critical projections, the scene's the opposite of ponderous with significance, or irony. The incident merely unfolds, growing out of an ordinary exchange, never declaring any special status or demanding any special consideration. Really, it's more like two characters in a movie quitting the script in order to beat the shit out of each other, more or less persistently, but with quasi-realist breaks to catch their breath, for six minutes.

The fight consists of two jokes, each without a punch line: its own bewilderingly formless duration *as* a movie scene—a joke that can't be punctuated, by definition, or it goes away—and the fact that Keith David would rather pummel and be pummeled than peek through the Hoffman lenses. If either of them stepped outside their entrenched positions to frame this absurdity ("You'd *really* rather keep at this than wear these glasses?" "You *really* want me to wear those glasses so badly you're going to take this endless beating?") the air of abjection and embarrassment would be hugely relieved, but the deadly serious joke lessened: here's another instance of Carpenter's willingness to lose your respect in order to consolidate your amazement and discomfort. If you hate the fight scene, you blame the director. If you love it, you credit yourself.

What's definite, anyway, is the extent to which Carpenter has now placed his bet on cult or folk transmission of what's he's got on offer, while excusing himself from the jurisdiction of middlebrow notions of "art" or "cinema" (*You can't fire me, I quit*). Sure, he once claimed to have cast Roddy Piper as an emblem of working-class authenticity, but that stalking horse has now bolted the ranch, in favor of what some members of a working-class audience (who'd say they've got more than enough "authenticity" in their daily lives, thank you) might be more likely to value: a WWF-style ass kicking.

Language more or less declines from the sort of arena that this alley has become—the characters reduced to grunts and squeals and asides like "Okay" or "C'mon" ("You *dirty* mother*fucker!*" is probably the screenplay's high point for these six minutes, and beautifully delivered by Keith David it is, too)—and film analysis finds itself shamed, too, if it knows what's honorable. Still, a few shreds of commentary may stand to be carved from the mayhem. One theme here is "valuables": Frank's motive for visiting Nada in his alley is to offer him "one week's pay. It's the best I could do," a wad of cash he chucks into Nada's box. Yet Nada, having seen a dollar bill decoded, doesn't even reach to pick it up—perfect measure of the gulf now stretching between these two. This note is sounded again when Frank bellows outrage at Nada's shattering of a parked car's rear windshield, the joke being that mangled and broken limbs are one thing, but, to Frank at least, the destruction of property another matter entirely. Nada, noticing this, laughs, making one of the fight's weirdly serene micro-interludes. Of course, Nada's obliged to panic when Frank threatens to stomp on the Hoffman lenses—that particular property ("the truth") being worth more than a week's pay and a car's windshield put together.

If we're not utterly race blind, there's a special poignancy at the lengths of Frank's resistance to the wake-up call. No white outlaw is going to tell this black worker how to protect his family! Frank defends a middle-class self-definition against a lower-order point of view, even if it's the truth. African-Americans might find that the view through Hoffman lenses offers an unbearable degree of indignity: Still a slave, fool. Still a fool, slave.

Six minutes really isn't the longest fight scene in film history if you count certain Roadrunner and Coyote or Tom and Jerry cartoons, which usually clocked out at seven.

Found Language Dept: odd proper names—DAKESSIAN, H. MADAT—are visible, stenciled on the alley's wall, indicating vacated parking spaces, reminding us that even this alley is only borrowed (film crew as homeless person!).

Roddy Piper's shirt is never untucked from his jeans.

In the end, it takes a thoroughgoing cynic to discount the tenderness that encloses the two men once Frank accepts the Hoffman view. (Were Howard Hawks and John Ford onto something after all, with all those tediously ribald beatings?) Staggering like partners in a sack race, Nada and Frank clutch at each other in consolation of their pain and fear, the god-awful injuries they've mutually inflicted standing in, irrational as may seem, for shattered illusions at learning what the ghouls have made of our world, and at seeing what few prospects remain within it for two squirrel-brained, oxen-hearted losers.

Fleabag Hotel

(1:02:05)

The arrival of the battered duo at the utterly persuasive flea-bag-hotel location is contrasted with the return of the score's mocking blues. The more things get real, the more they get cartoonish. Roddy Piper's quip when they check in to a private room to salve their injuries—"Ain't love grand?"—acknowledges the homoerotic subtext for anyone skeptical of the film's self-awareness, but on the diegetic level it's a cover for the discomfort over how intimate they've grown. (Men joke to push things away; films joke to bring them closer.) Frank, gazing out of the hotel's window, gets his own serene, high-angle matte-painted glimpse of architecture and ideology, a shot whose only moving part is a tiny blimp in the distance. Otherwise, it might as well be a black-and-white still, elegantly claustrophobic enough for Fritz Lang. Then Nada warns him about the headaches: "Don't wear them glasses too long."

Long Night of the Soul

(1:04:48)

In what may be *They Live*'s most anomalous passage, Nada, seated in a flea-bitten chair beside a hotel window flaring with the light of passing police cars, sips a beer and blabs. Gone into some kind of morbid fugue, he offers Frank a spontaneous abuse confession: during his boyhood, Nada's crudely religious father first baptized him at the river, then "turned mean," once even going so far as to hold a razor blade to his son's throat: "I said 'Daddy, please . . . He just kept movin' it back and forth . . . like he was sawin' down a little tree."

Listening sympathetically, Frank recasts Nada's ordeal in terms of Frank's own fresh revelation of ghouldom: "Maybe they've always been with us," he says. "Maybe they love it—seeing us hate each other, watching us kill each other off, feeding on our own cold fuckin' hearts." Nada, in turn, accepts Frank's conflation as a rallying cry: "I got news for them. Gonna be hell to pay. 'Cause I ain't daddy's little boy no more."

This discomfiting excavation of method-actor back story (whether factual or not, the lines appear to tumble out of Roddy Piper's interior motivational sump as much as Marlon Brando's childhood monologues in *Last Tango in Paris*) recalls one earlier moment: the despondency we glimpse when Nada meets the black junkie-squatter while hiding in the ruined apartment block. Given Nada's (and the film's) tidy reordering of his pain as a license to kill, what's suggested may be the reason why an action hero of his (traumatized, Rambo-esque) type must, like a shark, keep moving forward: to pause and rest one's brow upon a bed-buggy mattress is to wade into a slough of morbid recollection. There may be, according to *They Live*, only two or three things you can do inside such ruined rooms as these: watch television, take drugs, or recall childhood abuse—or, more likely, watch television or take drugs in order *not* to recall childhood abuse.

A Recent Scourge as Old as Mankind Itself

An elite is inevitable.   —Jenny Holzer, Truism

I'm not saying things were better *before*, I'm just saying they're worse *now*.

—Michael Seidenberg (in conversation)

"Maybe they've always been with us." This uncertainty, this "maybe," is a sort of undertow sucking at the toes of *They Live*. Our ostensible satire of the Reagan yuppie generation, specific in time and place, keeps gesturing toward corruptions of the human spirit and species as ancient as Lovecraft's Cthulhu, or some other force even more fundamentally Gnostic. So, when did the problem start? As far as specific dates go, the film is noncommittal, though it wouldn't seem necessary for alien invaders who'd been with us for more than a few decades to spend much time bragging about their recent growth curve, as these ghouls do. At deeper layers, here the film's employed a Keatsian "negative capability": that profitable anxiety set resonating in us at the levels at which we register the confusion. If "our own cold fucking hearts" are the matter here, then who needs alien invaders? (Like most of the best science fiction, the literal devices at some point threaten to resolve into "mere" metaphor.) And if the nightmare's intrinsic to human history, why such an emphasis on present regimes of consumer greed, dry-look hairstyles, and blue-corn tortillas?

Paging Slavoj Žižek! The Slovenian philosopher's conflation of Lacanian psychoanalysis and Marxist politics equips a viewer to consider the notion that human consciousness, forged in familial psychodrama, yearns innately toward totalitarian ideological control (the most recent incarnation of which, according to Žižek and Carpenter, is the inverted totalitarianism of late capitalism, with its injunctions to *consume* and *enjoy*). In other words, maybe Bad Daddy and Big Brother are more or less all one problem. Poor Nada's got an inkling; though outfitted only for rampage, his fury's more revolutionary (in Žižekian terms), not less so, for having bundled outrage at the ghouls together with recollection of both Judeo-Christian paternalism and his own father's monstrousness.

Something in the Water Does Not Compute

Through the critical ideological glasses we directly see what, with my psychoanalytic jargon, I would have called "the master signifier" beneath the chain of knowledge. We learn to see dictatorship *in* democracy. There is, of course, a naïve aspect in this staging, reminding us of the not-so-well-known fact that—some friends told me this in the 1960s—the leadership of the Communist Party of the United States, in order to account for its failure to mobilize workers, seriously entertained the idea that the U.S. population is already controlled by some secretly distributed drugs in [the] air, in [the] water supply, and so on.

—Slavoj Žižek, "They Live! Hollywood as an Ideological Machine"

SLIPPING INTO MADNESS IS GOOD FOR THE SAKE OF COMPARISON —Jenny Holzer, Truism

In Philip K. Dick's 1967 short story "Faith of Our Fathers," set in an Orwellian communist future, the lead character, a mild party bureaucrat, finds himself dosed with an unknown drug, one that leads him to behold a terrifying vision of their Great Leader as a tentacled, Lovecraftian monster. The drug he's taken is revealed to be an *anti*-hallucinogen: this regime has been keeping its citizenry compliant with a steady diet of hallucinogenic drugs. As in *They Live*, delusion is effortless, routine, and stable, while the "truth," acquired in some disreputable street transaction, is grueling, bewildering, and grotesque.

Dick, however, goes further: when the protagonist is recruited into a revolutionary cell populated by others whose vision has been disenchanted, he discovers another truth even more shattering: none of those who've taken the anti-hallucinogen see exactly the same monster. Only the delusions are in agreement; the "truth" is terrifyingly divergent, and therefore completely isolating. Dick's story then develops along religious lines, pointing to its writer's growing interest in Gnosticism: the supreme leader is in fact a kind of dark god, one who's imposed the delusions to shield humankind from an encounter with knowledge it could never withstand. The lies of repression are, here, more or less *an act of mercy*, at least from the point of view of Dick's (typically) meek protagonist. In the world of *They Live*, it may not be impossible to imagine other personalities, the opposite of Nada's and Frank's blustery, aggro-outsider temperaments, for which the Hoffman lenses would be worse than an unwelcome gift. The glasses give you a headache *at best*. At worst, they might open a void of rage, despair, and incomprehension beneath your feet, into which you can never stop falling.

The Futility of Collective Action

(1:07:42)

Gilbert enlists Nada and Frank in the resistance, which has reconstructed itself along somewhat more militaristic lines since being scoured from the church, and since the arrest or murder of its spiritual (preacher) and academic (hacker) figureheads. We're quickly moved through the substitution of contact lenses for the Hoffman shades ("there's less interference"), the reintroduction of a few minor characters (the white father and daughter from Justiceville, etcetera) and a paint-by-numbers speech from Gilbert ("the creatures are trading wealth and power . . . most of us just sell out right away . . . we'll do anything to be rich") on the way to rearmament for our two heroes and the reappearance of Holly. Frank is given a watch, ghoul property that will figure in his and Nada's escape a few minutes later. Really, all this organizing seems a bit beside the point, given the way *another* column of riot police is about to dynamite it all to bits. Has there ever been a less effective armed underground than this? Maybe Nada's a bad luck charm for collective action.

Carpenter's hero, Howard Hawks, claimed *Rio Bravo* (where John Wayne relies solely on a small group of experienced gunmen) was a rebuke to *High Noon* (where townspeople rescue Gary Cooper). What competent sheriff would ever really *want* the help of numbers of untrained civilians? Just protecting the common Samaritan might be more trouble than it's worth. Carpenter, too, seems to be gathering these well-intentioned but hapless bands together only to discredit them: what's needed is a lean commando unit, like the one Nada and Frank, forged in alley brawling, have melded into.

Holly is seductive in this scene, but she's surely sold out already—she's trying to shift suspicion from Cable 54, the station where she works ("The transmission is going out clean"). In retrospect, what we take for an attraction to Nada is just anxiety, as she tries to learn what he knows, and whether it puts her role in danger. Her soft-talking lulls us, and Nada, so that the explosion that launches the police attack is deafening.

Meet John Doe

> Now, real human social life is *tough* because in a demographic
> democracy you *never* criticize the subtext of your market.
> If fifty percent of your audience is made up of semiliterate
> farmers you do *not* set about to critique the manners and
> mores of semiliterate sons and daughters of the soil; you just
> work that semiliterate soil into your *style* and your *approach*.
> Now, in the America of *aujourd'hui* (and I promise you, this
> is true), a full fifty percent of our demography is made up of
> semiliterate sons and daughters of rock-and-roll—a fact *never
> to be mentioned* since it is sacred *subtext*; i.e., what the *New York
> Times* needs to be cognizant of (and silent about) now.
>
> —George W. S. Trow, *My Pilgrim's Progress*

Mike Judge's *Idiocracy* (2006), a satiric excursion into an
American future where the average I.Q. is 45, culminates (for
the time being) a science-fiction meme: *The masses are getting
intractably stupid, wow*. The roots are H. G. Wells's *Time Machine*, with its Morlocks and Eloi, but it was probably Cyril M.
Kornbluth's 1951 short story "The Marching Morons" where
contemporary media critique got folded in: *They sure will buy/
watch/believe anything, won't they?* With its anti-corporate gestures and television satires, *They Live* dabbles in *Idiocracy*'s turf
(like a lot of eighties sci-fi films, *Robocop*, *The Running Man*).
But Nada's a Common Joe, isn't that the whole point? Unlike

Idiocracy's protagonist, he's no time traveler from a smarter future. He's a representative man, a fine bit of rabble.

They Live's ambivalence about the masses—their ingenuous salt-of-the-earthiness, their pathetically passive manipulability—has loads of good company in Frank Capra's vibrantly incoherent celebrations of common humanity: *Mr. Deeds Goes to Town*, *Mr. Smith Goes to Washington*, *Meet John Doe*, *It's a Wonderful Life*. Capra (in his person as politically vague as John Ford, or John Carpenter) compulsively celebrates the massed power of indigenous American folk against the Machiavellian operations of elitist politicians and journalists, except when he's compulsively excoriating the herdlike, proto-Fascist gullibility of mobs of ill-educated fools, those who time and again must be protected from their own impulses, before they destroy the gift some self-sacrificing hero (i.e., Gary Cooper or Jimmy Stewart) has magnanimously provided. The tensions in Capra's films—isolationist American heroes wading into the compromising morass of urbanity—are the same that the Western traditionally puts to its back, by pointing its heroes West. Carpenter, under pressure, resolves his urban story in the manner of a Western: Nada's caregiving responsibilities are passing phases, his chances of lasting affiliation persistently wrecked. (Whether by some flaw in his character or not, you decide.)

Another Alley

(1:14:41)

Big difference: last time Nada and Frank were present for a ghoul raid on resistance headquarters, the two, in ducking for cover, became stranded from each other. Now, hipped to ghouls, armed and dangerous, solidarity forged in the alley earlier, the white guy and the black guy make a brave stand in another (but do lose track of Holly, who wanders through the gunfire like a sleepwalker). Nada and Frank mow down a satisfying number of ghoul troopers—for a moment, *They Live*'s a war movie. Then a neatly crafted camera movement (dolly in from the ghoul point of view, alternating with a dolly out from Nada and Frank's) pins them in this alley's cul-de-sac.

War Movie, Science-Fiction Movie

(1:16:14)

It takes ghoul technology—the time-slowing, teleportation wristwatch—to rescue Nada and Frank from the alley. Their plunge into the mysterious ghoul manhole evokes, again, like the garbage truck did, the archetypal outlaw-hero's requisite passage through sewers and shit. This hole turns out to be more of a multidimensional portal, however (like the "ten thousand holes in Blackburn, Lancashire," from *Yellow Submarine*); no sooner have Nada and Frank become effective guerrilla commandos than they're shifted into the most wheezily traditional science-fiction sequence in the film (complete with gobbledygook alien font on the signs on the walls of the underground tunnel, and the laboriously unnecessary interstellar-travel device). Genres won't sit still for these poor guys.

Human Power Elite

(1:17:58)

> The notion of an establishment seems to be a social fairytale,
> a deadly utopia or invisible system that inspires an almost
> mythical sense of dread—it is a "bad dream" that has some-
> how consumed the world. I shall postulate The Establish-
> ment as a state of mind—a deranged mind, that appears
> to be a mental City of Death . . . Everything that is the
> antithesis of art rolls on after brainless slogans: "Everyman
> is equal—the war on poverty—win the mind of man to
> freedom"—all echo into the poisonous skies.
>
> —Robert Smithson, "The Establishment"

The windowless ghoul ballroom, wreathed in Kaopectate-
pink drapery, proves the mediocrity of the ghouls' notion of
the rewards of privilege. Here we've reached *They Live*'s Heart
of Darkness—shouldn't the human power elite, for their trai-
torousness, be lavished with something more decadent, more
elitist, more goth-ostentatious, perhaps like the orgy scene
from *Eyes Wide Shut*? If heaven is a place where nothing ever
happens, this is something a great deal worse: we can project
a succession of grindingly dull speeches like this one we're
briefly privy to, the sort given at conventions of minority corporate shareholders, congratulating them as this speaker does,
on the growth of their "per capita income." The room surely

reeks of mothballed tuxedos, tepid banquet chicken dinner, and carpet cleaner, a place very much "the antithesis of art," and which Carpenter unmistakably loathes as deeply as he does airports (in Milan Kundera's memorable title phrase, "Life Is Elsewhere"). Yet again, a handful of ghouls are seated at the tables, presumably masquerading themselves among the members of the elite—they're slumming, here! One female ghoul rears her head in laughter, delighted, as if this occasion were more than just something to endure with gritted teeth. For our part, we're relieved Carpenter finds nothing to linger over here; the setting's barely established before being interrupted by the reappearance of the one sort of human who might be forgiven for finding this sort of occasion to be something genuinely enviable: the formerly homeless Drifter.

Drifter's Escape

(1:19:07)

> "What's the threat? We all sell out every day, might as well
> be on the winning team!"
>
> —Drifter

In stories where characters align on simple axes of good or
evil, the most interesting are those who vacillate, oscillate,
or otherwise delay or complicate their affiliation. In *Casablanca*, Victor Laszlo is noble, Major Strasser is vile, but Rick
Blaine is where the action is. In the twentieth-century, post-
Freudian, post-Virginia Woolf sense in which we've come
to define a good fictional character—capable of tragic error,

three-dimensional, psychologically rounded, whichever term you'd prefer—these nonaligned, diffident, or treacherous characters often feel like the "modern" characters in an otherwise "pre-modern" (allegorical, mythological, biblical) narrative structure. To what degree such characters (and their decision-making processes) are placed at the center of a story might be one of the easiest superficial indicators of how seriously a work is intended (or, anyway, how seriously it is likely to be received). If Shakespeare had written *The Lord of the Rings*, its title would be *Gollum*.

They Live features two examples of new recruits to the human power elite—Holly and Drifter—both of whom make their realignment offscreen. Holly's is by far the larger role, and the more instrumental, but her journey through the tale is also murkier, veiled in notions of female passivity and allure. It's as though Carpenter has placed us in Nada's shoes: *he* doesn't get this chick, and neither do we (in this case the glasses just don't work). Drifter's betrayal, on the other hand, is laid bare, so that even Nada may easily grasp it and be disgusted. "I knew you and me had a lot in common, first time we met," Drifter tells Nada, but Nada just stifles a sneer: this turncoat is as wrong as the ghoul cop was when he claimed revulsion was a two-way street.

Drifter exists in the story, really, to serve as betrayal's personification (well, that and as a kind of half-assed science-fiction tour guide, in the *Forbidden Planet* tradition, giving vague summary of the wonders of ghoul-tech: "some sort of gravitational lens deal—bending the light, or some damn thing"). The tasteless revamp the former homeless raconteur's been given—tux and coiffed hair—begs the question of what possible use Drifter's been put to in the ghoul's schemes for world domination. Paul Nelson once quipped of Joan Baez, "What does she have to sell out?"; it's hard to imagine that at the ghouls' first job fair the position of Fatuous Cocktail-Swilling Jackass didn't have willing applicants lined up around the block. Yet apparently there's always room for one more.

Playing on Drifter's vanity, Nada and Frank are ushered into Cable 54's stronghold, where, Drifter explains, the "master signal goes out from here to the satellite. We pump it out all over the world." Nada, his disgust barely concealed, walks with right hand gripping his left forearm, a posture made legendary by John Wayne in *The Searchers* (though credit is always paid backward, to Harry Carey), and therefore encoding embittered and sulky resistance to social conformity. (In Nada's case, it may also be useful in concealing a large pistol in your underwear.) When Nada and Frank unveil their firearms, killing two ghoul guards at the threshold of Cable 54's newsroom, Drifter seems truly astonished at their naïveté. "You still don't get it, do you, boys? There ain't no countries anymore, no more good guys. They're running the whole show. They own everything, the whole goddamn planet, they can do whatever they want!" Nineteen eighty-eight is pretty early for this nascent anti-globalization jab. Naomi Klein's *No Logo* was more than a decade away, though demonstrations at the 1988 Berlin meetings of the International Monetary Fund were a precursor to the then-unnamed protest movement. *They Live* can't claim responsibility for the Berlin scuffles, which occurred six weeks before the film opened.

Drifter stands for all we're meant to despise most, and he's squarely in Frank's and Nada's sights—so why does the film let him use his ghoul wristwatch to escape, squirting away with a mocking, "See ya, boys"? Maybe this is Carpenter's nihilism surfacing: Drifter's sleazy opportunism is the cockroach of the human spirit, not so readily snuffed out, fascinating for its versatility and endurance. (Carpenter, in an interview, credited Drifter's "we all sell out every day" remark to a Hollywood development executive.) Or maybe we've detected here a sneaking fondness for the sniveling bastard. Drifter's a loner-provocateur, one who works the margins (he wasn't actually *seated* at the banquet); in that regard he's not so far from a Carpenter hero like Nada after all. And thus, unlike Nada, Frank, or Holly, he's allowed to live another day, could even be eligible to appear in a sequel. Maybe it'll be called *Drifter*.

Inside Television

(1:24:09)

Television is reclaimed as a prominent subject matter in the last ten minutes of the film, but now the motif's turned inside out. Earlier, televisions were seen as having injected themselves into our world like an alien virus. Now, Nada and Frank have invaded the immune system of television, in order to expose its artifice and shatter the monolithic hold of its signal. The bumbling Cable 54 newscasters aren't far from the *Saturday Night Live* caricatures seen on the broadcasts earlier in the film, but now they're real characters in front of us; helping television impose a cartoon on reality, they've become cartoons themselves. Carpenter's delight in exposing the feebleness of the set from which TV news generates its authority reminds us of how, earlier, a reel-to-reel tape recording stood in for the rebel church's parishioners. In his low-budget film about cheapo illusions, Carpenter teases us for being cheaply fooled.

Workplace Shooting

(1:24:33)

Features clotted into a mask of prole rage, Nada leads Frank on a rampage through a backstage area full of production assistants or assistant producers (how could we ever know the difference?), some of whom are ghoul, some human. Our heroes murder the ghouls, leaving the humans to run screaming from the scene or crouch keening in terror inside pasteboard cubicles, essentially defenseless. The grim certainty with which Frank and Nada navigate, combined with the utter helplessness of the humans to protect themselves or even know what's at stake (since they're not wearing lenses) makes it uncomfortably easy to reverse the polarity of the scene. Here's what a workplace shooting might really feel like: grim slayers choosing, by some inscrutable logic of their own, between doomed victims and those fated to survive.

Around the next bends of their journey, Nada and Frank confront wide rooms full of cubicles, manned by humans who obligingly flatten themselves to the carpet or simply stare in paralyzed disbelief at the guerrillas in their midst. In recent decades we've grown wretchedly accustomed to the testimonies of those who cringed beneath desks or slipped into supply closets, waiting out school or workplace massacres—techniques of survival handed down, made familiar, by the testimonies of other survivors. Who knows, some of us may, in the manner of airplane passengers measuring the distance to the over-wing exits, have identified an emergency route or sanctuary cubby, a fallback position for that day when the crazy wrestler and his black friend barge in and start shooting the joint up. Or do you identify more with the civilian folk hero, he or she who tackles the maniac gunman and pins him to the floor until the SWAT team arrives? Nobody like that works at Cable 54.

Sympathy for the Ghouls

But Vader also seemed absurdly trapped in his throatbox and his cloak of gloom. He prowled around self-consciously, almost, it seemed, wearing his mask in public shame, or wearing his shame in the form of a mask. It was as though he was too discreet to show himself, perhaps out of simple reluctance to inspire repulsion. And, as many suspected and was finally confirmed, all he was really hiding was a maimed face. I always had an inkling, watching him stride around in glum determination, that Vader wore the mask because he was vain, and chose to inspire fear rather than repel desire. Alternately, I speculated, maybe his face was not awe-inspiring at all. Maybe it was just a plain face with a flattened nose, a weak chin, and rabbit teeth. Maybe Vader needed the mask because without it he was just a man you passed casually on the street . . . It seems to me sometimes that I am surrounded by Vaders. The Vaders are the ones who do not wear their hearts on their sleeves, who protect themselves from exposure. They do not display themselves in all their weakness to disarm would-be detractors, adopt a deceptively submissive pose to fool fearsome opponents. They do not broadcast their flaws, do not reach out to others by seeking and embracing a communion of weakness, of understandable frailty . . . Vaders do not make inappropriate remarks at dinner parties, let down their guard in drunken

The ghouls chosen to die in the television station are dressed in pastel sweaters, carrying clipboards and wearing headsets; they raise their hands with civilian gentility as they try (pathetic in a way we can too easily imagine being pathetic ourselves) to outrun or flinch from the automatic gunfire, further emphasizing their humble proximity to the human lives they're meant to be exploiting so ruthlessly. Nada and Frank have gone military, but these dying ghouls aren't soldiers. They're office nerds, "little people," very much like the film crew presumably working for scale to hush the set and adjust the lights and fix the continuity between the takes of Carpenter's shoot. The film's scenes of routine ghoul intermixing—the beauty shop, the bank, the grocery store, leading up to this pedestrian work environment—have migrated through horror, revulsion, and pointed satire to achieve a kind of drab inevitability: They Live, sure, and so do They schlep, file paperwork, get stuck on hold, and work fifty weeks for a two-week vacation. They're just as much the kind of "normal fucking people" (the words of Harry Dean Stanton in Alex Cox's 1984 *Repo Man*) that hipster filmmakers either shower contempt on or box out of the frame from sheer disinterest. Wouldn't you rather be Drifter, half-assing his way through the banquet, than stuck in here fetching coffee for a Cable 54 executive? For that matter, wouldn't you rather even be

Drifter *before*, in his raffish hat, pontificating in an open-air parlor? Drifter's fourth-billed, after all.

Carpenter keeps pushing some intolerable subject toward visibility here, but he can hardly bear to keep it in view himself. The cold hierarchy of moviegoing attention mimics the cruel triage room of consciousness itself: we turn our heads for heroes and deciders, those at the centers of stories, those who help us believe we're the centers of stories ourselves. The rest are extras, chosen not for their glamour, but for their innocuous capacity to get small tasks accomplished without demanding any particular attention we might not find it easy to spare. Then, sometimes, we need them to die. To be honest with ourselves, don't we hate the ghouls not so much for their Jacuzzis and Rolexes, but for the soul-sucking compromises needed to earn those perks, for the plodding acquiescence of their days, for their lives of quiet desperation? Really, why don't a couple of these ghouls go on a rampage?

"By forty you have the face you deserve." So said (the ghoulishly gorgeous) Abraham Lincoln-like Nada, a man of the people who took an unmistakable lead role as emancipator and martyr. That's it, then: blame the victim. These ghouls aren't suffering selves (when they die, or when they sigh); they're allegorical unpersons, here to remind us of how much more complete *we* are inside the unmelted skin of our own yearning, self-marveling, narratively central selves (even if our own particular fifteen minutes as protagonist haven't arrived yet). *We* never plunged greedily, face-first, into the cheese dip, only to find we'd surrendered our native humanity and natural hairstyle, to find we'd thereupon need to rely on a cheap wig and a obfuscating broadcast to put ourselves across, to even be allowed to mingle and play among the real people, the okay people, the people like *you*.

Pregnant Secretary with Coffeepot

(1:25:04)

The last gratuitous detail *They Live* makes time for is an
amusingly stymied, very pregnant secretary who steps into
the corridor clutching a two-thirds-full coffeepot, her wad-
dling stride on perfect collision course with the frantic Nada,
who then conducts a gentle and useless interrogation of the
tongue-tied woman. The poor dupe is searching for Holly.
Like the depressed Latina maid, the pregnant secretary is
placed at Panavision's far edge: a pan-and-scan editor would
be forced into atrocious choices between her and Frank, who
stands on the other side, exhorting Nada not to waste time
(Frank even whispers "Who's Holly?", unclear on the narrative importance of the woman who'll murder him three minutes later).

The pregnant secretary is played by Eileen Wesson, daughter of the ubiquitous 1950s comic character-actor Dick
Wesson. Eileen's barely an actor, according to IMDB.com;
these ten seconds are her only film role in the whole decade of
the eighties, and she didn't work again until 1997's *Mystery
Monsters* (in which she's billed as "Mom"). Yet she imparts a
grain of comic brilliance, if only in her walk (or maybe pregnant woman just walk funny). Nada and this woman seem to
regard each other across some impossible gulf: her dopey humanity, her polka-dot dress, the coffeepot (which, like a detail

from Jacques Tati, echoes her stomach's bulge): she's from another movie, another world. Much like the bumptious comic reconciliations toward the end of *The Searchers*, all of which serve to strand John Wayne's character even farther inside his own revenger's exile, this cameo encounter highlights Nada's unsuitability for the domestic sphere. He really *shouldn't* be looking for Holly—he's got no knack with women. The pregnant secretary's still visible, standing bemused with her coffeepot held high, comically still in the midst of swirling panic, as the soldiers thunder through her corridor at 1:26:12. She's a small precursor to Frances McDormand in 1996's *Fargo*: a pregnant woman as a rebuke to masculine mayhem.

Tiny Alphaville Homage

(1:26:35)

Godard's futuristic allegory *Alphaville*, which divides human-kind between the computerized drones of Alphaville and the still-passionate humans of the Outlands, bears comparison to *They Live*: for one, both make no-budget science-fiction sets out of crappy modern architecture. At *Alphaville*'s climax, as Eddie Constantine abducts Anna Karina from the clutches of her dystopian city, several enthralled citizens are seen groping through corridors, clinging to the walls as if blind, or blind drunk. For an instant, *They Live* nods to Godard's iconography (black-and-white courtesy of Hoffman lenses, of course).

Holly Kills

(1:27:15)

When Holly appears, and the three make their final push for the rooftop, the camera subtly favors Frank, as though helping us make a small farewell, or making its own. Holly's cool as a cucumber, and Frank, having manfully iced any number of ghouls and their soldier-accomplices on his way through the building, will never know what hits him (in fact, we'll cut on a flash of light as Holly holds the gun to his temple, saving on gore and a close-up squib effect). It's as though genre backlash has crept up on these guys once more—who'd been warned to look out for a femme fatale?

Any way you slice it, Frank's execution is a bummer. If you're tempted to ask why it has to be him, rather than Nada (Frank could as easily do what Nada will: reach the roof, take out the satellite signal, and flip the bird to ghouls everywhere—and probably in superior style) you're opening a can of worms: might as well ask why we couldn't have parted ways with Nada from the moment Frank agrees to put on the glasses. This movie was never about the black sidekick, don't kid yourself.

Rooftop

(1:27:56)

Nada abides with the completely unremarkable satellite dish for a quiet instant, before a Hoffman-lensed shot shows us the queerly humming 1950s sci-fi mechanism from his point of view. A pay-dirt smile plays on his lips as he trains his weapon. Then Holly appears behind him, weapon also trained, husky wiles shamelessly enlisted for one last pitch for ghoul accommodation: "Don't interfere. You can't win." On cue, helicopters float up from below, satanic apparitions. Holly drops her voice another register, adding an unmistakable sexual enticement to her admonitions: "Come inside with me."

She's right: Nada can't win. He's Nada, after all. Yet, since *sometimes Nada is a real cool hand*, he also can't lose in trading his life for the death of that ghoul-signal-generating dish. The remaining minutes of the film (all two of them) are sheer nihilistic exultation: not only the spark-showering explosions and the giddy wrenching off of the ghoul-masking device worldwide, but the fatal gunshots themselves, which bring a kind of release as we're shed of the burden of Nada and Holly as characters we're meant to hope to see connect and prevail. No, no, no, it was never going to be that way, not for them. Holly falls rather like a Nosferatuan vampire rising in reverse;

breaking with Nada's meticulous precedent, she's his first civilian-human kill. Nada takes his own mortal bullet with a wrestler's stoical grace, that of a career loser—no Andre the Giant, he—handed a typical script of defeat yet unexpectedly being granted life until the final reel.

In Living Color

(1:29:56)

The next sequence, showing the effects of the rupture of the ghoul-masking signal, goes by so quickly that, on first viewing, it may seem more extensive or complicated than it is. First:

Resolving out of a glitch of static as the masking signal recedes, male and female ghoul newscasters, seated before a wall marked, simply, TV, carry on reading a transitional blurb while their horrified crew, glimpsed as blurs in the foreground, groan and scream and quit the scene. ("Gloria, you look like shit!" says one guy, sounding that note of disappointment at female-ghoul-ugliness we've heard from Nada.) For what it's worth, these *aren't* the Cable 54 broadcasters from 1:24:09, who presumably were human. But they're equally dorky and clueless. (When ghouls are unmasked, ghouls are seemingly the last to notice.) The channel changes:

Here, ghoul-Gene Siskel and ghoul-Roger Ebert are seated on a set that brandishes a prominent NO INDEPENDENT THOUGHT backdrop. Ghoul-Gene Siskel fatuously condemns movies like *They Live*: "All the sex and violence on the screen has gone too far for me—" Cut to:

A ghoul seated at a well-populated bar, dressed in an ill-fitting, Steve Martin-esque white suit, drinking alone among humans, and gazing up at an unseen television, which

plays the ghoul version of *Siskel and Ebert at the Movies*, as above. Ghoul-Gene Siskel continues droning in voice-over: "I'm fed up with it. Filmmakers like George Romero and John Carpenter have to show some restraint. They're simply—" Carpenter's self-congratulatory rebuke to (real) critics hasn't sat well with critics of the film—it isn't taken, for instance, as a wry metatextual joke in the manner of a Hitchcock cameo. Yet the joke is in tune with the relieved, expulsive tone of this final sequence, in which various modesties are thrown giddily aside: narrative conventions, a brassiere, and so forth. The bar's patrons respond with rising horror to the ghoul in their midst, who's either very slow on the uptake or pathetically hoping to ride the moment out (*Maybe they'll eventually learn to like me for who I am*). Following the logic that we're at last seeing the ghouls plain, with no assistance needed from glasses or contact lenses, ghoul colors now blaze: mostly blue, with red and white blotches and highlights. The hues of a chunk of deeply rotten carcass. This mournful bar ghoul is the one seen reflected (with image flipped) in the glasses of

They Live's poster. He's Ghoul Prime, and he's drowning his sorrows. The channel changes:

We've returned to the kind of "found footage" montage (whether found or manufactured isn't actually obvious) typical of the film's first half hour, but vertiginously fast: a glossy model backed with neon (two seconds), a sports car's headlamp flipping up from its hooded position (one second, or less), a spotlit rock-and-roll drummer pounding his sticks in a trance of ecstasy (a few frames). Cut to . . .

The End

(1:30:21)

John Carpenter closes 1994's *In the Mouth of Madness* (another tale of a skeptic who discovers that his world has been corrupted by an evil fiction) with the protagonist settling into a front-row seat at a movie theater, for a screening of *In the Mouth of Madness*, the movie we've been watching all along (cf. *The Muppet Movie*). *They Live*, which begins in prosaic documentary style, in some ways begs to be a film that ends lost in artifice. We might, for instance, cut away to another vacant lot, another version of Justiceville, where another batch of tatterdemalion couch potatoes sit vacantly gazing at a television's screen. On *their* screen, we'd see the final instants of Nada's "triumph"—his killing of Holly; his destruction of the broadcast tower; his epochal, dying flip of the bird. The homeless viewers would hoot and cheer, then change the channel. Life goes on. Cue hollow laughter.

    They Live flirts with this impulse. The post-Nada montage, Ghouls Unmasked Worldwide, nearly comes to a close not in the arena of the real, but instead lost within the kaleidoscopic maze of commercial simulations, that hall of mirrors that might truly reveal monstrosity, if we ever locate our glasses. Instead, Carpenter plunges us back into something both more and less real, this smutty kick at the finish. He's found one last destabilizing swerve, one last fuck-you gesture. The director might be toying with the ratings system (or the Gene Siskels of the world): *Looking for a new definition of the word* gratuitous? *I'll take an "R" for the last shot in my film, thank you.*

Or he might be toying with *us*. The girl and ghoul don't really feel like they derive from the same version of reality that earlier defined this film, a quasi-documentary on disenfranchisement. These two are lost somewhere in the breach between the TV satires and their own longing for authentic contact, *fucking with the TV on*, or *watching TV with the fucking on*, their behavior mediated through porn stylistics that have invaded their sexual imaginations (the human woman's "cowgirl position," her regimented moaning, his "baby") to an extent *They Live* simply can't help them unmask. And we, complicit (male) viewers, noticing ourselves twitch to hard-wired attention at one flash of tube-boob, thinking *Was it that sort of movie all along? Do I owe someone an apology?* (A brief, ridiculous cut-in shows a human woman gasping in censure as she slaps the face of a male ghoul, who then turns to the camera as though shocked by the site of bare breasts, making him the first unmasked ghoul to begin to grasp that *the jig is up*—and is he somehow looking through the screen?) *Can we freeze that frame a second longer? No?* Oh well, roll credits. Cue mocking laughter (and an obnoxiously taunting, discofied version of the score's blues motif). We're stranded here, at the end, women handcuffed to men, in bed with the pun/chline's verdict: *We're all fucking ghouls*.

Grade: B+

> [I]n order that men should resist injustice, something more is necessary than that they should think injustice unpleasant. They must think injustice *absurd*; above all, they must think it startling. They must retain the violence of a virgin astonishment.
>
> —G. K. Chesterton, "The Vote and the House"

I think that the degree to which the film appears xenophobic depends rather heavily on one's relationship with the rest of the culture. For many of us film lovers in urban areas, the extremist tendencies of middle America are not only frightening but deeply distasteful, something to which we would prefer to close our eyes. After Waco, after the stand-offs in Montana, after Oklahoma City, after the Unabomber, the disenfranchised of America appear to coastal sophisticates as a gun-happy, Bible-thumping, multi-pronged terror, protective of its racial purity and distrustful of outsiders. And in such a context, Piper's stabs at comic book bravura might remind us of our worst fears. However, if one holds an image of poor Americans as people betrayed by their own country and prone to extreme responses, then *They Live* becomes a different film, the one modern action epic with a genuinely proletarian hero . . . Most films are "ideologically incoherent," as are most people. The coherence usually comes in bursts, singular impulses and ideas. *They Live* is a film made out of sadness and anger, both of which it sustains right up to its mordant final shot. And now, in 1999, it's a film whose contexts—societal, political and cinematic—have disappeared. Which makes it even more precious and vital than ever.

—Kent Jones, Turin Film Festival catalogue, 1999

Chaplin has always seen the proletarian under the guise of the poor man: hence the broadly human force of his representations but also their political ambiguity. This is quite evident in this admirable film, *Modern Times*, in which he repeatedly approaches the proletarian theme, but never endorses it politically. What he presents us with is the proletarian still blind and mystified, defined by the immediate character of his needs, and his total alienation at the hands of his masters (the employers and police).

—Roland Barthes, "The Poor and the Proletariat"

Pink Floyd, *Animals* (Columbia, 1977) This has its share of obvious moments. But I can only assume that those who accuse this band of repetitious cynicism are stuck in such a cynical rut themselves that a piece of well-constructed political program music—how did we used to say it?—puts them uptight. Lyrical, ugly, and rousing, all in the right places. B+

—Robert Christgau, *Rock Albums of the '70s*

FIN

NOTES

Epigraphs

Christopher Sorrentino, e-mail to the author.
Andrew Hultkrans, e-mail to the author.

Note on Approach I

The four books on my desk: Gilles Boulenger, *John Carpenter: The Prince of Darkness*; Robert C. Cumbow, *Order in the Universe: The Films of John Carpenter*; John Kenneth Muir, *The Films of John Carpenter*; Ian Conrich and David Woods, eds., *The Cinema of John Carpenter: The Technique of Terror*. *They Live*, as you'd expect, is the subject of abundant entries in directories of cult/science-fiction/horror film, as well as innumerable blog posts, many of which are worthwhile: my favorite is Letter to America's "Relax and Shop: John Carpenter's They Live Is a Documentary," which presents an amazing photograph of an airport sign reading RELAX AND SHOP—it's to this blog that I owe the comparison to *Full Metal Jacket* (see note on "Bifurcation," below.)

Note on Approach II

"known generally as a 'cult' film": *Rain Man* was 1988's eventual box-office champion, though it never won a week in 1988; the money was collected in 1989, after the Oscars. Other successful 1988 films included *Beetlejuice*, *Twins*, *Coming to America*, *Who Framed Roger Rabbit?* and, the winner the week before *They Live* opened, *Halloween 4: The Return of Michael Myers*—connection to which John Carpenter disavows. *They Live* was the top-grossing film the week of its November 6 release, then faded, a commercial "disappointment."

NOTE ON JARGON

"diegesis": I like Wikipedia on *diegetic* a lot: "'Diegetic,' in the cinema, typically refers to the internal world created by the story that the characters themselves experience and encounter: the narrative 'space' that includes all the parts of the story, both those that are and those that are not actually shown on the screen (such as events that have led up to the present action; people who are being talked about; or events that are presumed to have happened elsewhere)."

LOS ANGELES PLAYS ITSELF

"blasted rise": This is the same default parkland on which Michael Douglas is ambushed by Chicano teenagers in Joel Schumacher's *Falling Down* (also featured in that movie's poster), a film of urban disquiet set in an *acknowledged* Los Angeles, and that had the strange luck of having its filming interrupted by the 1992 Rodney King riots.

GRAFFITI AND TEXT ART

"Sometimes it was as simple as": Jenny Holzer, interview by Patrick J. B. Flynn, *The Progressive*, April 1993.

puns on Roddy Piper's career: Here's Piper, from an interview with "Mecca Don": "Andre and I go way back. I had over two hundred matches with Andre the Giant. I was one of the few people that did what I wanted to do when Andre was around, other than push Andre around. Andre took me under his wing, as did many other old timers. And I was the only man ever to have Andre the Giant bleeding, carried out on a stretcher in Madison Square Gardens [*sic*]. That's what Andre thought of me. What do I think of Andre? I don't think I've ever met a finer human being."

Auteurs within Auteurs

"Based Upon the Short Story 'Eight O'clock in the Morning'": Long ago, I used to see Ray Nelson at science-fiction conventions in Berkeley. He was a droll and bright-eyed elf of a man, and known for wearing a propeller beanie, regarded as a high talisman of fannish identification, the equivalent of an IT'S A BLACK THING, YOU WOULDN'T UNDERSTAND T-shirt. I felt in awe of Nelson's lingering traces of involvement with Philip K. Dick, my personal hero, and he, Nelson, always struck me a figure of absurd dignity, brandishing his two or three secret accomplishments through an otherwise invisible life—in Berkeley in the 1980s, he didn't even rate as an eccentric, he was apparently too mild. I was terrified of becoming this man.

Television Made Me What I Am

Monolith Monsters: Identification of this footage courtesy of Roger C. Cumbow.

It's remarkable, once you begin to tabulate it, how routinely, in the 1950s, Hollywood's insecure distaste for television was reinforced. In Vincent Donohue's 1958 *Miss Lonelyhearts* (a film taking the disingenuous manipulativeness of the newspaper medium as one of its prime subjects), Montgomery Clift, seeing his nephew propped on elbows before a TV Western, sneers, "Educational television!" Everyone knew what he was talking about.

Assorted Hoffmen

"Setting your open-ended conspiracy metaphors loose upon the world": According to *The Conservative Journal* website, my novel *Chronic City* ranks with Glenn Beck's *Arguing with Idiots* and Sarah Palin's *Going Rogue* as one of the "Top 10 Best Books of 2009."

Villainous Vehicles

"who directed Stephen King's *Christine*": Carpenter and King are of a generation that also threw up "Duel" (a faceless big rig) and "Killdozer" (guess what?).

The Next Six (or Eight, or Ten) Minutes of Film

"falls back to earth, exactly when?": My friend Michael and I used to be obsessed with the problem of discerning the last worthwhile gag in Blake Edwards's *The Party*. The film, a Peter Sellers slow-motion farce of serial humiliations at a stuffy Hollywood party, is perfectly poised for its first hour or so, but ends with a gratingly goofy cavalcade of hippies giving a psychedelically painted baby elephant a bubble-bath in a swimming pool (a very 1960s way for a poised farce to go wrong). It seemed to us that if we were addicted to repeat viewings of *The Party*—we were—we should be able to identify the exact moment when the film turned the corner, and hence when we were justified in turning it off. Eventually we surmised that the fatal "last gag" was Sellers's superb pratfall off a shingled rooftop. We were certain of it, in fact. Yet Michael and I always found we wanted to stick around for a verbal exchange that came after, where Gavin McLeod shouts "You're meshuggah!" and Sellers, misunderstanding, barks back: "I am *not* your sugar!" By that time we were so close to the end that we always ended up seeing the elephant anyway, and then we'd surrender, and go through to the final credits. But it was nice to feel we'd figured it out.

Cheap Sunglasses

"novels of Bret Easton Ellis": Bret Ellis and I were students at Bennington College in 1984–85; I remember him having a poster with the jacket image from Costello's *Trust* taped to the wall of his dorm room.

Bifurcation

"What Hitchcock does, in effect": David Thomson, "David Thomson Revisits 'Psycho's' Critical Moment." By Michael Fox. SF360, December 14, 2009.

Kubrickian strategy of halves: *Full Metal Jacket*'s second half, featuring scenes of suspiciously effortless wish-fulfillment violence by its boy-soldiers (alternating, of course, with their humiliations, and tormenting deaths), while also showing them posing for and being interviewed by television crews, makes an interesting comparison with *They Live*'s lack of self-consciousness about its vicarious component—unlike Kubrick's soldiers, Nada and Frank never consider the possibility that they're being televised.

Fight, Fight

"A fabulous movie": Greil Marcus, e-mail to the author.

The End

"pun/chline's verdict: *We're all fucking ghouls*": John Hilgart, e-mail to the author.